IGNITE GLOBAL CHANGE

*Creating innovation
in low-resource settings*

Alessandro Crimi

T0386225

R^ethink

First published in Great Britain in 2024
by Rethink Press (www.rethinkpress.com)

Disclaimer

To my parents, Carmelo and Marianna

Thank you for the gift of life and the education you gave me, ultimately leading me to acquire the knowledge I am passing on with this book.

To David, my son

I will always be there for you when you need me, despite the people and circumstances trying to keep us apart.

To the unborn daughter from a Finnish mother

Life is just a phenomenon you sometimes cannot control.

Contents

Foreword

This book magically synthesizes the diverse building blocks of social and entrepreneurial innovation in Africa. While I raced through the preface of this book, I was hooked on and felt like coming back to its pages. Every chapter had some magic to it and resonated with my personal experiences as a student-turned-founder/ecosystem builder who was involved in catalyzing socially inclusive communities for new biotechnology adoption in Africa and living the talk by building the first 'open biology makerspace' in Ghana to develop the tools needed by scientists in low-resource environments to enable access so they can confidently pursue their research curiosities.

This book isn't just for entrepreneurs and innovators, but it's a must read for everyone.

Harry Akligoh, Northeastern University, founder of Duplex Bioscience and initial cofounder of the Kumasi Hive Biolab

Introduction

You are in Accra, Ghana, where the sun kisses the earth, pineapples and coconuts are everywhere, and ancient rhythms pulse through its people. Sometimes it is hot, but sometimes it is even hotter. Here, a new generation of unstoppable dreamers is rising. Meanwhile, in Mumbai, whistles resound in traffic jams, cows are considered sacred animals, and a level of obsession with Bollywood and IT degrees exists. In this rainbow of apparently unrelated things, the icing on the cake is highly skilled engineers and businessmen. Nevertheless, in these places, life is not easy, competition is strong, and entry barriers for young game changers are considerable.

These scenarios are not isolated to exotic places. Even if you live in Europe—let's say London, Paris, or

Milan—the lifestyles are different but the challenges are similar. If you are a young scientist, finishing your PhD, with ideas that you want to convert into reality, you will look like Don Quixote against the windmills. Italian policies impose huge taxes to establish new companies, and only well-settled companies can survive. Life is also hard here—trust me, I tried.

Our world is run more and more by algorithms, and we are almost innovating in real time. Self-driving cars, machine-learning-designed drugs, nanotechnologies, computations running on quantum devices, and so on. You probably have ideas that can help society with these or other technologies, but how to translate these ideas into a stable business, association, or something else out in the world is a real pain. Also, all those innovations need to be sustainable, meaning long term. As an entrepreneur or activist you need to create something with the resources available, considering costs and impact on the environment and society.

I managed to obtain degrees, including a PhD, an MBA, and others. However, relevant knowledge is often found in non-academic books, taught by mentors, or learned by doing in the real world. I had some success in projects in sub-Saharan Africa and some disasters costing venture investments.

I am an academic, and I am used to looking for strict evidence and data. According to the World Bank, there are still eight countries where more than 60% of the population lives below the poverty line.¹ While United Nations reports say that in 2021 nearly USD$2.15 billion in investment capital was directed to the tech startup sector in Africa.²

I am also an entrepreneur, and I like to do things in the real world and not be trapped inside an ivory tower. I have worked with non-governmental organizations (NGOs), other scientists, bureaucrats, activists, and mythological creatures originated by the crossing of them. I have been at venture capital (VC) meetings, at academic conferences, and in bumpy, dusty roads where water is at the forefront of your mind. I have seen how things fall apart when the wrong cofounders or partners join you in projects. I have observed people working day and night with little guarantee of a return of investment in the near future, and I have had several "aha" moments while talking with people or reading books. I talk to community leaders, sparking changes with every activity or business venture they embark upon. This is mostly the result of many years of studying, trying, failing, and succeeding.

Do not be scared—this is a world filled with limitless options. Dreams are everywhere, but without the proper mentorship, dreams can remain just dreams or can lead to failure. Pivoting and mentorship are highly important. I did not want this book to be just a guide; it is more a testament to the grit and resourcefulness that defines young activists or entrepreneurs. Indeed, I summarize books I have read, tricks I have seen people doing, and lessons I have learned in my own skin.

You, the entrepreneur or activist, exist within a larger society; you are not the center of the universe. With the first part of this book, I want to give you a broader view – a theoretical summary of what is wealth, why certain countries got rich, and why others were stuck in poverty. Part One also contains a summary of previous policies that failed, and shows us what we are left to do as individual citizens. Then you can move on to how we can find useful ideas, and how we can unleash our creativity and empower our team to find solutions within our society.

In Part Two, I want to give you practical advice about how to move in the real world. You will hear relevant practical issues that they do not teach you at business school—which you will learn on the way—and sometimes, if you do not care about these, they can lead you to fail.

Part Three is also practical but oriented to technical solutions in the computational world, and how to access them if you have little financial resources or you are in the southern hemisphere.

As we do not want to leave dreams just as dreams, we will focus on a roadmap to turn ideas into reality. We are talking of creating wealth from almost nothing.

It is possible, but there are no magic tricks. Ultimately, it comes down to your own responsibility and effort.

As you flip through the chapters, you will learn certain tricks that allowed people to move from their garage to the rest of the world – practical, annoying, but necessary aspects such as positioning, marketing strategy, survival, and exit strategies. I hope you will find this advice useful or, who knows, even life-changing.

To have long-term strategies, we need a fundamental change in how we view innovation. We need more focus on sustainable problem solving and design thinking over specialized technological advancements. Let this book be the catalyst that ignites your passion for innovation, inspiring you to embrace change, leverage collective wisdom, and embark on a journey of boundless possibilities.

PART ONE
FROM POVERTY TO PROSPERITY

We must be honest; the world is unfair. If you are born into a rich family or in a "first world" city, your chances to create a something are not the same as if you are born in a slum in Nairobi. Likewise, if you are just a PhD student in biotech and do not have any knowledge of economy, influential connections, or quality relationships. Before we delve into practical advice and case studies on how to create wealth with your association, company, or government, let's revise a couple of fundamental questions.

There are unfair advantages in our society—why do they persist? What is wealth? Why are some countries stuck in a loser loop? Above all, from where do we start to create something useful? Where do we find ideas that can be put into action in the real world, given this background?

Let's answer these questions. Chapter 1 revises most common theories and ideas about wealth; Chapter 2 delves into more recent approaches for economic development; while Chapter 3 moves into starting solutions from the bottom up.

ONE
Wealth And Predicaments

This chapter features policies that relatively failed. This is a little abstract, but we need to realize that as activists or entrepreneurs, we are just a part of society. It starts defining what wealth is and how it is measured, and points out the reasons why certain countries or contexts lag behind. It will also revise theories that have been proposed yet have never fully solved poverty or promoted wealth, assuming the top-down view. The next chapter moves into more contemporary approaches to economic development.

Wealth creation

What is wealth? Is it dollars or bitcoin? For an ascetic, wealth is given by the ultimate currency: happiness unrelated to material possession. However, few people follow this approach. Wealth is a multifaceted concept: it's more than just having money. True wealth comes from having financial freedom as well as rich relationships, abundant resources, good health, and time to enjoy those things. It is about having security and options in life. Often in history this multifaceted concept was tied to specific objects, which in turn influenced health and human relationships.

In the early stages of mankind and for some rural communities (even nowadays), wealth was and is cattle. In the Ethiopian Empire, before the introduction of the birr, blocks of salt called *amole chew* served as currency. Other goods have also been used at other times, such as tobacco, oil, gold, and copper.[3] Therefore, wealth is perceived as being acquired or obtained through the ownership of specific material assets. Nevertheless, those goods might lose value over time. For example, after salt was replaced by other substances to preserve food, it lost its value and nowadays nobody thinks of it as something like gold.[4] Wealth depends on the value someone attributes to a specific thing at a specific time.

Currently, for the majority of the population of planet Earth, wealth is measured in money, in one of many valid currencies. If you think about it, this is just a number on a piece of paper. How can a piece of paper be so important? Even more so if we consider the digital age, where money is not even tangible but is a number spread all over information technology infrastructures. How can those abstract things be so relevant? They are relevant because at a specific point in time we all agreed they were relevant—they form a social contract.

A further question is: "How can wealth be increased given a small amount of material assets?" If we understand this, we can use our insights on how we can more effectively use education, health, and other policies to improve the quality of life in our communities. Economy refers to the production, distribution, and consumption of goods, and this can be seen as a unique dynamical system,[5] highly complex with microscopic elements that allow the emergence of overall states of wealth for certain populations. It is not possessed by a single person or several people, although some people might have a bigger share than others. Everything is a network; we evolve exchanging ideas and goods. If you want to get rich, you need to connect to people who are willing to spend money on your products or services. Moreover, if you want to do something new, you need to introduce perturbations or spread new ideas through the network. Sadly, the network sometimes has resistance to change, and limits the introduction of more environmental, affordable, and fair solutions—we will come back to this later.

Even though we are all connected and live in a huge network, historically we have subdivided it into subnetworks that we call countries. You should imagine yourself as a node in one of those subnetworks, and your family and friends other nodes—we are all connected. The most common way to quantify the wealth of those countries (subnetworks) is through their gross domestic product (GDP). According to the Organisation for Economic Cooperation and Development (OEDC), the GDP is "an aggregate measure of production equal to the sum of the gross values added of all resident, institutional units engaged in production,"[6] and these also include taxes.

GDP is a way to quantify the economic performance of an entire country, but it is a bad measure because it is an average. If you are in a bar full of people on low wages, the local GDP will be low, but if Bill Gates enters, on average the GDP will be high, however the wealth is unequally distributed. Substantially, GDP is a common measure but it's less representative than we think. To overcome this limitation, we have introduced other concepts, such as the Gini Index and the Human Development Index (HDI).

The Gini Index, named after the economist Gino Corradi, is a measure of statistical dispersion intended to represent the income distribution of a nation's residents. Absolute equality within the country is indicated by 0 and complete inequality is given by 1. According to data from 2008–09, African countries have the highest pre-tax Gini coefficients. Among them, South Africa ranked the worst with the world-wide highest coefficient valued between 0.63 and 0.7.[7]

The HDI is a value composed by different estimates, such as life expectancy, education, and income, used to classify nations into four groups according to an overall human development status.[8] The introduction of the HDI is related to the belief that increasing GDP does not necessarily reflect the increase of well-being and happiness of a population, and perhaps different views of what is development should be considered.

Why am I telling you this? To ask you to think again in terms of what development is, and to understand that statistics and other reported facts are often oversimplifications; they do not allow you to think about what we can do. A more balanced, psychological and holistic approach is required. If you are a policy maker, you should look at the behavioral aspects of people, not just at summarized numbers. If you are an activist or entrepreneur, think again. Later in this chapter, why we need to go beyond these simplifications will become clearer.

In the way we measure wealth independently, there is no general recipe to make a country rich or poor; each country has different situations and cultures that empower and limit beliefs. What worked in one country might not necessarily work somewhere else.

Nevertheless, there are several factors influencing why certain countries become rich; some of them are passive and some are active. Although the passive factors are given by nature, our attention should be on what can be changed. Yet, there are countries that have been considered poor but have made it through to becoming more developed. Why? What are the core aspects that led them to improve?

Poland and Singapore are good examples of countries that have transitioned from being relatively poor to more developed economies. As someone who has visited both countries, about fifteen years ago and recently, I have witnessed firsthand the massive improvements in infrastructure, technology, and overall quality of life. Katowice train station in Poland is now a modern building attached to a huge shopping mall, including luxurious branded shops, similar to Bahnhofstrasse in Zurich. When I saw it in 2006 it was a gloomy postcommunist place where you would hardly pass by, even during the day. Krakow fifteen years ago barely had a bus network and a couple of trams; now you can easily use a combination of trams with USB chargers, buses, and short-distance trains that minute count down to the stops (comparable to what I have seen in Switzerland) and free Wi-fi. How did this change happen in just fifteen years?

Let's assume we ignore history before the fall of the Berlin Wall. If you look at Poland in 1990 you can see it had a GDP per capita (apologies for using the GDP) of USD\$1.731, while in 2023 its GDP is USD\$18.321—an increase of more than ten times in just thirty-three years.[9] Similarly, Singapore's GDP was USD\$11.862 per capita in 1990 and USD\$82.808 in 2023.[10] Even though we know GDP is a biased indicator for an entire population, those indicators suggest that, overall, those countries have made developmental leaps that other countries at similar starting levels did not manage to achieve, as depicted in the figure below. This can be attributed to several factors.

Poland's market economy saw a major turn for the better. After the fall of communism in 1989, Poland transitioned from a centrally planned to a free market economy, allowing for private enterprise, competition, and foreign investment. This stimulated economic growth. The country moved from state-owned to privatized enterprises slow enough to be transparent, improving efficiency and innovation in former state industries. (Even I work for a major technological hub in this country.) New private businesses also emerged. Moreover, Poland joined the EU in 2004, creating a profitable access to larger export markets and EU development funds to build infrastructure. It also led to institutions and regulations that supported growth. Lastly, there was a focus on education reform and training to build up its skilled workforce. This supported a shift to more knowledge-intensive industries, avoiding the middle-income trap.[11]

Similarly, Singapore oriented its economy around exports early on, rather than domestic consumption. It attracted foreign investment and built export hubs. The government pushed technological adoption and created a welcoming environment for businesses with low taxes, good infrastructure, trade agreements, sound regulation, and openness to immigration. Also, in Singapore, the focus on education was strong. Singapore invested heavily in education to develop human capital. This created a highly skilled and tech savvy workforce.[12]

In summary, both countries owe their economic rise to market-oriented reforms, education, adoption of technology, and policies that attracted investment and enabled enterprises to flourish. Applying human effort, ingenuity, technology, and resources to produce things people want is how new wealth is created in the economy. Can everybody do it? Unfortunately, yes and no. What is going to happen if you are an entrepreneur or activist in a country where the government does not carry out smart moves like in Poland and Singapore?

Let's discuss the factors to identify the culprit and the solutions. Who is the knight of honor and the evil dragon of our story? Who knows? Maybe you—the activist or entrepreneur detached from the government and institution—are the knight of honor.

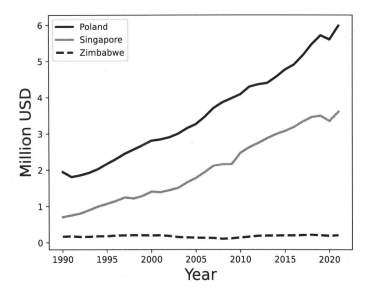

Total GDP for Poland, Singapore, and Zimbabwe over time. To obtain the GDP per capita, the total GDP has to be divided by the same year's population.[13]

Geography, resources, or institutions?

Living in a land with a lot of salt or gold, or a nice climate allowing easy agriculture, are passive factors. Passive factors have a considerable impact on achieving wealth, but they do not necessarily grant it. The industrial revolution occurred in England because of the vast coasts, innovation such as James Watt's steam engine, and supporting institutions.[14] Coastal proximity is important, as in those days, boats were the main vectors to sell goods; indeed, many cities arose along rivers or coastlines. If a country did not have coastal proximity it was limited and doomed to failure. However, Switzerland has no access to sea and no more rivers than other European countries. What is their secret?

When other countries with a lot of resources, a pleasant climate, and favorable circumstances, had a climactic moment in their history, they then experienced economic crisis for several years. Did Argentina improve in the last thirty years? Did Italy? I have been regularly visiting Palermo in Italy, my home town, and I have noticed no improvements in infrastructure in some parts of the city in the last twenty years—literally nothing. How is it possible that certain countries with fewer resources regenerate themselves and others that have a lot of resources are struggling or even moving downward from high-income countries to almost middle-income countries?

The answer is simple but hard to manage: bad governments. A good government is capable of reverting a negative condition and putting their own country on track, while a bad government can do the opposite. Therefore, even if geographical position, weather, and resources are important, institutions and government fulfill a more important role. Let's not be populist so easily; governments are often the mirror of the local culture. Don't start just blaming your government or institutions.

In *Why Nations Fail*,[15] Acemoglu and Robinson provide a more complete analysis by showing that the
most influential elements to the wealth of a country
are likely to be the institutions and their derivatives.
Let's take a closer look at their best example, the cities
of Nogales and Nogales-Sonora.

The two Nogales: one in the US and one in Mexico[16]

As depicted above, Nogales-Arizona and Nogales-
Sonora are attached cities belonging to two different
countries. Nogales is in the US—more specifically,
Arizona—and Nogales-Sonora is in Mexico. Their climate is the same; if there are airborne diseases, they
spread equally in both cities; and inhabitants are
mostly descendants of common ancestors.

Arizona's Nogales has an average local income of USD$30,000 a year, and local inhabitants generally hold at least a high school degree. Most of the citizens are relatively healthy with access to Medicare.[17] Despite it not being the most popular and wealthy area of the US, the standard services and institutions are set and they are not so different from the rest of the US.

In Nogales-Sonora, sometimes called Heroica Nogales, the majority of adults do not own a high school diploma and many teenagers do not attend classes. High rates of crime are recorded, and starting a business is a dangerous endeavor. Additionally, there is little support when opening a company and the consequent risk of necessary bribes is high. There is a straightforward explanation as to why these twin cities are different: their governments. Arizona's Nogales relies on US economic institutions, while its Mexican twin is in an area that was under the control of the authoritarian Partido Revolucionario Institucional until 2000.[18] If you want to start a business, the number of hurdles you will meet highly depends on which side you live—a few kilometers can change your life radically.

This is not a coincidence or an isolated case. Look at the two Koreas: North and South. Or compare Botswana—which had liberal democracy since gaining independence in 1966—and the attached Zimbabwe under dictatorship for ages. The first has among the highest per-capita income in the sub-Saharan region, while Zimbabwe... well you probably heard about it, remains among the most impoverished countries of the planet, while actually having even more resources than Botswana.[19] This is the so-called resource curse.

The resource curse is a well-known phenomenon characterized by a negative relationship between resource abundance and economic development,[20] mostly related to bad governments or interest groups. This paradox of plenty is particularly pronounced in countries rich in natural resources, particularly non-renewable resources like oil, gas, minerals, or other valuable commodities, often experiencing negative economic, social, and political consequences. This is mostly because the local government relies excessively on those resources, ignoring other possibilities or investments. It can also be caused by misman-agement, corruption, and foreign companies taking advantage of the circumstances. Instead, a way to fight the "curse" is given by sharing the benefits fairly between private and public sectors and by better allo-cating public budgets to improve spending on basic healthcare and education, tackling inequality, and generating employment for poor people,[21] so, once again, it is related to the local institutions.

Culture

It is not just government. There is evidence sug-gesting that there may also be a correlation between progressive policies or culture in general and wealth in a country. For example, Japan and Germany are ranked as the most progressive countries culturally and they also rank highly in other indices, such as GDP, Gini Index, and HDI.[22] These rankings indicate that progressive policies, for instance in areas such as gay and women's rights, may contribute to a country's overall success and wealth. This suggests that countries or contexts where more progressive cultures are predominant may also be ahead in terms of social justice and equality. This might ultimately positively impact the local economic development.

When I was living in Denmark, I noticed that chief executive officers (CEOs) of companies—my boss or other high-profile figures—were dining during the lunch break, even sitting at the same table of other employees, without flaunting their status. Obviously, there was a hierarchy and packing order, but this was emerging in specific moments, not as a general behavior. Living in other countries afterwards, for example France and Switzerland, I noticed the opposite. It was what I later know to be the "power distance index" (PDI). The PDI is the measurement of the acceptance of a hierarchy of power and wealth by the individuals from the general population of a nation, group, or company.[23] It is a concept developed by the Dutch social psychologist Geert Hofstede.

Interestingly, countries with a smaller PDI tend to be more progressive and more prone to development[24] as subordinates challenge the authority of the person or people in charge more easily. "Challenge" does not necessarily mean to create a riot or a "French revolution," it might just mean to introduce a new business model that is not typical for the local culture or to address your superior if something is not working. Ideally, institutions are inclusive and provide equal opportunities to all members of the society they are in charge of, independently of their social status and background. This might create a friendly environment, fostering innovation and encouraging economic growth.

Religions (or lack of them) are part of the local culture, and in some cases are the most influential aspect. Therefore, they can have a large impact on the development of a country. Indeed, religions play a significant role in shaping the values, beliefs, and behaviors of individuals and communities.[25] This in turn influences the development of a country in various ways. One trend that can be observed is the potential influence of religious values on social cohesion and community development. Many religions promote certain ethical principles and moral values that can contribute to a cohesive and harmonious society. The general message is: "Love thy neighbor."

In some cases, religion might push dogmatic thinking, which is anti-liberal and conservative, creating a hostile environment for innovation. If a country does not have institutions conductive to economic success and instead is reinforcing dogmatic values, we run into hurdles. If you are a young PhD student with an idea but live in a country with an unfavorable culture or long power distance, and approach a bank for a loan or a VC company, you might not be taken seriously, since cultures with large power distance are tendentially risk adverse. If we are in a condition of power to change these institutions, we should act, reducing power distance and introducing wealthier circumstances through new policies.

We cannot conclude that the correlation between progressive policies or culture and wealth is necessarily a direct causation; it might rather be a reflection of the overall values and attitudes of the country. Yet, local culture and beliefs have an impact on the open-mindedness of people. It is not just the government, it is the culture overall. Therefore, if you are born into a highly conservative context, you might find more resistance while introducing "changes" in society. Do not be discouraged; it simply means that things are like this, not that you are wrong.

In summary, natural resources and geography are important, but the government is the main reason. If you are a policy maker reading this and you do not create favorable conditions for your people to thrive, create businesses, or activities, you need to realize that you are the main reason that your country is poor or underdeveloped compared to others.

Is your country like this and you are not a policy maker? You need to realize things can be hard. You have three options:

1. Emigrate to where there are more favorable situations

2. Figure out what the tricks are that allow you to thrive, circumventing all hurdles in your society

3. Privately fix all lacking infrastructures by substantially doing the job your government is not doing, which you include in your financial plan

The first solution is the easiest, but we do not discuss it here. Instead, we focus on the other two, though the latter might require considerable financial investments.

If we do not have policy-making power and we are just a small NGO, businessperson, or research institution, advanced problem solving and new approaches are required, which I will discuss with you throughout this book. You need to know the tricks to overcome the hurdles of society, using channels that are not under the control of your country's governments or institutions. You need to think outside the box. For example, do not plan a distribution or supply chain in your own "unfriendly country," but export to other countries. Or go fully online and do not rely on local logistics. If your local tenders are too lobbied or corrupted, you need to focus on EU or international foundation calls, and so on. Obviously, these are for the moment just abstract examples; I will go into more practicalities later.

Social traps

Look at the figure below. It represents the combination of the income you have one day and next, which depends on a certain asset you have. Let's say it is given by two cows you use to get and sell milk. This is your main job, not a hobby and there are also some expenses linked to costs, such as maintaining a barn and other fixed costs. Unfortunately, the amount of milk you sell leads to little new income and slowly you need to reduce the cattle cake, with consequently less milk, then reduced income, and then you lose your cows (in the figure, you are the arrow moving toward the left). It is as if your income is always decreasing; starting from the top arrow, you go downward each day, almost to zero.

Now, let's imagine a different scenario. The government gives you two additional cows, so you now have four. You start selling more milk and you slowly grow (now you are the arrow going to the right in the darker space), until you have a stable income and the income of today is the same as the day after but relatively high. These kinds of situations have often been called "poverty traps,"[26] in the sense that given certain

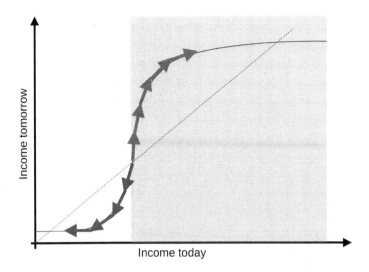

The S-shaped curve depicts the poverty trap – each point represents the combination of today's and tomorrow's earned income. Down towards the left is the path of someone starting at a certain income and then being trapped in poverty. Up towards the right is the path of someone escaping the poverty trap, heading toward a stable income.

circumstances, you are trapped in a specific income level or can even go down in income, and with just your means you cannot escape this situation.

The S-shaped poverty trap curve depicted in the figure above should indeed explain the phenomenon where individuals or economies get stuck in a cycle of persistent poverty. This graph suggests that there are certain thresholds that, once crossed, can have either positive or negative effects on poverty and economic development.

It has often been debated whether poverty traps even exist, or if they exist only in circumstances of extreme poverty. Nevertheless, it cannot be denied that there are situations where instead of growing, we enter a downward spiral. For instance, if you have a startup and instead of getting clients you bury yourself with fixed costs, then you start making cuts to limit expenses, those further cuts reduce your visibility and therefore clients, and you know the rest of the story. Your startup will behave like the two cows scenario, with less and less milk each day.

Another example might be if you end up unemployed. It could happened to anybody at some point in life. You have been searching for employment continuously for months. You are struggling to pay your bills, despite the fact that government aid programs have helped you pay for rent, utilities, and food. Finally, you read an email about a job application you submitted some time ago. The interview goes well, and you are hired. When you receive your first payment in a while, everything begins to improve; the storm is over and you finally see the sunshine. Unfortunately, you are just looping in the left side of the above figure. The new job earns just enough to keep you out of benefit programs, but barely enough to cover the same costs as before. As a twist of fate, you have less money now than you did when you were jobless, since you have to cover commuting and other costs. This dismal situation is often called the welfare trap. You might think that poverty or welfare traps are easy to solve, but they are not. When a large share of a country population is living these circumstances, the country or region itself can be stuck into a trap.

Jeffrey Sachs is an American economist and director of the Earth Institute at Columbia University. For Professor Sachs, a poverty trap refers to a cycle that prevents individuals or communities from escaping poverty due to various interconnected factors and mechanisms. One key factor of the poverty trap is the lack of access to basic resources and infrastructure. In impoverished regions, there is often a scarcity of vital resources such as clean water, healthcare facilities, education, and transportation. This hampers the potential for economic growth and development, trapping individuals and communities in a state of poverty.[27] Indeed, a trap is characterized by self-reinforcing mechanisms that perpetuate poverty, leading to countries remaining poor. The poverty trap is often described as a spiraling mechanism that forces people to remain impoverished, with limited opportunities for upward mobility.[28] To address the issue, research focusing on identifying policies to break the cycle has been carried out.

According to Sachs,[29] the solution should simply be given by national or foreign aid supplying the initial capital to allow individuals to escape from this trap. This has been the major approach by humanitarian and developmental organizations, such as the United Nations Development Programme, World

Bank, and governments in low-income countries since the year 2000. Did it work? Apart from cases like the aforementioned Poland, Singapore, or Rwanda, not really. Otherwise, African countries would now be like Switzerland. In the next section, we will discuss this. Scholars even explain that this solution hampers development even more, as they create the opportunity to waste aid or leave people in the limbo described below.

Welfare programs are even trickier because they involve the psychological decision of whether a person should work or stay on their program. People living in those programs are encouraged to continue receiving government help if they know that working will not increase their net benefit. People work, of course, for a variety of factors, such as cultural expectations and moral principles, and some might become depressed if they are not working and are still receiving an income. It generates a feeling of not being useful in society. However, a primary driver for seeking a job is for income to cover expenses.

Limiting the welfare state or totally removing it would be cruel, creating a harsh society. A basic income might stop people from being poor in the first place by establishing a steady income level below which no one can slip. However, this approach has been fought rather than adopted by the majority of policy makers. The only way to start ending the cycle of poverty is to give people the capacity to make lasting changes in their communities and lives, not just by throwing money to create Hamleting circumstances: to get welfare benefits or not to get benefits?

The vicious cycle of aid and no growth

We can now put the social traps ideas together with what we discussed in the two Nogales example. If a country does not have a strong presence with progressive policies, is there a chance that providing funds will be ineffective due to the likelihood that funding will be wasted? Dambisa Moyo, in her provocative book *Dead Aid*,[30] advocates this. Foreign aid and Western politics are actually guilty of hurdling development of African countries and other low-income countries in Asia and South America.

Developmental foreign aid is actually contributing to the problem, not the solution—an idea that is also widely supported by well-known economists such as William Easterly, who talks about the "tyranny of experts."[31] According to those views, aid prevents people from developing their own solutions, while corrupting and undermining local institutions. If the poverty trap is a never-ending loop, foreign aid is also a self-perpetuating cycle between lobbies of aid agencies. Therefore, the best chance for developing nations to escape those hypothetical poverty traps is not to get more aid, but to rely on free markets where individuals may find solutions to their issues on their own.

Despite the good intentions, systemic aid has been fostering corruption within inefficient governments. This waste also makes a country or region unattractive to foreign investors who are not willing to start their businesses in a non-transparent context. This is a situation also experienced in Europe – for example, in Sicily due to the "pizzo" tax that the local mafia used to ask companies for when establishing their businesses.[32] Although it can be debated that corruption is actually an indicator of growth, lack of transparency seriously interferes, reducing economic growth and employment. No economic growth will require new systemic aid, so the story starts from the beginning again. Foreign aid fosters corruption, foreign aid blocks exports, but, above all, foreign aid creates dependency.

In fact, a country or a recipient used to receiving money easily is not prompted to promote entrepreneurship or inner production, which leads to no innovation. No innovation will promote what again? The need for aid. Another chicken–egg loop that is hard to break. This is the welfare trap described at the beginning on a country scale. It is necessary to break the circle, promoting innovation in the country and avoiding the use of foreign aid. For an NGO or a company, these solutions are not under control and the choice is to use problem solving to survive and prosper, even in these unfriendly circumstances.

I am afraid I have confused you. Is external help a good or bad idea? Why does a minimum income guaranteed by the state sound like a good idea when it might not work as well?

Summary

Aid alone will not work; changes have to be embedded in empowering initiatives. What do we do if our country is not providing decent policies, and all the best institutions do is create welfare traps? The answer is in the following chapters, but first we need to delve into other aspects, often neglected by economists, such as behavioral economics, evolutionary economics, system thinking, and randomized controlled trials.

TWO

Contemporary Economic Development

In this chapter, we continue the top to bottom view but attempt a more critical look at economic development with contemporary approaches. The next chapter is more about what we can do and how to start looking for solutions, given the difficult environments in which we live.

Poverty is a complex problem

It is the morning of 19 October 2019 in Sweden. Esther Duflo and her husband Abhijit Banerjee are employed at the Massachusetts Institute of Technology, and they are probably sleeping due to the different time zone. They will receive the news later. The Swedish

Nobel Academy has awarded them the Nobel Prize in Economics for helping to develop an innovative experimental approach to alleviating global poverty. Nobel Prizes are usually the culmination of a life's work or attributed to a specific innovation. The couple have conducted several studies related to poverty – most of them in India and South Asia. Among their research, I would point out two major aspects: the "clinical" approach to developmental issues and behavioral economics.[33]

The previously described approaches have noble starting points, yet the optimistic view of Jeffrey Sachs, the negative views of Dambisa Moyo and William Easterly, and even the basic income rule are relatively anecdotal. Those policies focus on simplification of complex human nature at a one-dimensional point. Moreover, they are not scientific; at some degree the welfare state, the tyranny of the experts, and the basic income theory are more hypotheses without rigorous scientific evidence.

In medicine, to validate an idea we run case-control studies. It means we take two groups: the case group and the control group—these are matched by age, sex, and other factors, but they differ for a specific factor related to a hypothesis—and compare results. For example, if we want to show the association between vitamin D deficiency and increased risks of diabetes, hypertension, cardiovascular disease, and cancer in the elderly, one group of elderly people will take a vitamin D supplement (case) and another group will not (control). After a period of time, we look at the statistics of health complications and verify whether the group taking the supplement had fewer of them. There are further aspects to take into account, such as the fact that often the researchers are blinded from which group they are studying—who is with or without the supplement—so they are not biased, trying to find symptoms in the group who is not taking the supplement. We often use the word "random" to indicate that subjects are taken randomly from a population. We should validate socio-economic policies in the same way, rather than the guesses of economists supported by politicians.

Indeed, there are examples of governments implementing policies, for example Mexico's *Oportunidades* anti-poverty program[34] was modeled as a randomized control trial, but these are exceptions rather than the rule. Obviously randomized clinical trials are not flawless; we can have false positives, false negatives, results can be limited to the sample of observation, and sometimes people manipulate data and processes to confirm their biases. As a quote attributed to Winston Churchill states: "Democracy is the worst form of government—except for all the others that have been tried."[35] Randomized control trials and case-control studies are not perfect but they are the best attempts to be objective we have so far.

Behavioral economics

To design impactful policies we need to understand the complex lives of the poor, and there is another universe that has been neglected by humanitarian and developmental experts called behavioral economics.[36] For example, there is a belief that people on low incomes do not care about health. This is totally false. Poorer people are tight with funds and therefore they try to do smart moves. Spending money in preventive actions when there is no issue is not seen as a smart move and often ends up as the opposite, as cheap preventions avoided for year might result in larger problems that require expensive cures. Why would you buy a new bed net when the one you have still looks good, even with a few holes? You might get lucky, or within weeks you could catch some mosquito-borne disease.

I myself had a similar issue. I was in Ghana, and I prolonged my stay for a project. I did not have enough anti-malaria pills for the last day, and due to stress I forgot to sleep with a bed net and to buy new pills. What could go wrong in just one day? After all, I had been fine for weeks. After one week back in Zurich, Switzerland, I started showing signs of malaria. I had to be treated and checked for weeks. Even with my insurance healthcare in Switzerland, it was expensive. I could simply have avoided that with one pill costing about USD$0.50.

Here is another example: poor families frequently allocate their entire education budget to just one child in the hope that this child will finish secondary school, while underfunding their other children. This happens because many families believe that spreading the family's educational expenditure among all their children would be a waste of money instead of focusing on getting one child to the top, introducing the idea that parents think in terms of "quality over quantity." Assuming this is actually true, or even that certain parents do not focus on education at all for—according to them—well-motivated reasons, investigating different random trials of families in South Asia, it was possible to identify the most successful policies. These were deworming and explaining to parents that the return of investment in education is tenfold. This helped more than financial incentives, as it deeply altered their decision-making over their children's education.[37] A proven change of behavior can be more effective than a blind welfare payment.

Imagine a welfare policy giving some people financial assistance. Do you think they would spend the money wisely? Some will, some will not. All of us wants something for status; we are all stupid in some degree. You do not want to appear behind so you need a mobile phone, and sometimes if you are poor you neglect to buy quality food because you spent money on an expensive gizmo. Therefore, to cancel poverty is not as simple as "giving money to the poor," as claimed by Sachs. There are a series of psychological issues that we should take into account, and communication campaigns to be set. Economy is psychology; it is not just policies and numbers.

Example of randomized controlled trial economical intervention

We can now together design a hypothetical case-control study in the style of Abhijit Banerjee and Esther Duflo:

You and I come across Santosh while researching poverty in Hyderabad, India. Santosh is a street vendor selling vegetables in a slum in the city. He grows some vegetables in his little garden then sells them from a movable cart in the slum, where residents have limited access to fresh produce. After asking him how much income he can generate, he replies "about 200–300 rupees a day," which is barely enough to support his family.

We decide to run a randomized control trial to test the impact of two simple interventions on Santosh's earnings. We talk with Santosh and we select other ninety-nine similar peddlers and run the following interventions:

1. We give a large colorful umbrella to twenty-five vendors to provide shade and make the carts more visible from a distance.

2. We give a simple folding table to another twenty-five vendors to display the vegetables neatly in rows.

3. We give both an umbrella and a table to another twenty-five vendors.

Hence, we randomly assign the umbrella, table, both, or none (control group: no intervention) to respectively 25% of the vendors across the city. We then track the vendors' earnings over a month using daily self-reports.

We find the vendors who received the table saw earnings increase by 20% (30 rupees). The umbrella had no impact alone, but the combined effect of the table and umbrella together was a 30% (60 rupee) increase.

This reveals that a simple, low-cost intervention like an organized display table can meaningfully increase the earnings for vegetable vendors in slums. The colorful umbrella acts as an amplifier. These insights can inform poverty alleviation programs and enable data-driven policies to improve livelihoods.

This hypothetical fictional case study uses Duflo and Banerjee's approach of using randomized trials to scientifically test low-cost interventions that make a difference in the lives of the poor. This field experiment demonstrates how small details matter and provide specific, actionable steps to address poverty.

Dear policy makers, next time you set something, remember to do it scientifically as a clinical trial, rather than according to your gut. The behavioral economics aspect would be to understand why the table attracted more sales. In the startup world you can do something similar.

Evolutionary economics

Paying attention to people's psychology is one of the most insightful methods, but we might end up going into anti-reductionism and miss high-level interactions on our planet. At the same time, I have already mentioned that oversimplification, such as the GDP, can lead to missing relevant details. A possible trade-off is to model the system dynamically, taking into account complex interactions.

Each of us is a node in a complex network with dynamics such as spreading ideas and exchanging goods. Those spreads generate continuous change or better evolution. An individual is not alone; he or she is generally part of an organization, country, or ethnic group. There are cultural evolutions through this network, as certain ideas—if they do not serve the purpose any more—are abandoned. Science is a good example of ideas that arrive, evolve, and are eventually replaced by something more appropriate.

It is the same in economics; we witness literal evolutions as in the biological sense. If you are a startup, you generate new ideas and new products; some will catch on and some will die. This is similar to genes showing mutations; some useful, some harmful, and some neutral. Only those that are useful will be carried out by individuals and will survive. There is a strong affinity between biology and economy. We can imagine that, like in biology, we have processes of differentiation, selection, and amplification. In business we have processes that differentiate, select, amplify business models, and spread across the system. This is the view pioneered by Eric Beinhocker in *The Origin of Wealth*,[38] and later reiterated by Matt Ridley. A typical sign of prosperity is specialization, while a sign of poverty is generally given by a lack of specializations. When people cannot trade their specialization for other goods or skills and have to rely on themselves, there is little room for innovation.[39] I am not saying that self-sufficiency or autarchy is a bad thing; it is a sign of poverty when people are limited by this.

It is also essential to have diversity inside the economic system. A variety of firms, industries, and people ensures adaptability and resilience to shifting economic situations. Diversity may be fostered and poverty can be decreased by policies that encourage inclusivity, equitable access to opportunities, and support for small and medium-sized businesses.

Economic systems must be able to overcome obstacles and adjust to shifting conditions. To do this, policies must be adaptable enough to take into account changing economic situations. People can be better prepared to adapt to shifting work markets and lower their risk of poverty by supporting policies that foster skill development, education, and training. This is a never-ending scenario, as in biology, we never stop evolving.

If you are not a policy maker, what can you little entrepreneur or activist do? As we said, diversification is the key element. It boils down to finding a new niche and diversifying, moreover remembering that the system is dynamic: you have to keep moving and evolving. A good niche or solution now might be suicide tomorrow. It is worth pointing out, your startup might be like one of those genes that is not useful during evolution and will eventually die out. The difference is that if you fail, you can acknowledge the issue and "think of another gene" startup, or pivot your idea. In the next chapter we discuss how to find a better product-market fit, allowing more survival.

Interest groups

The reason why certain policies fail can be related to many factors, such as imperfect design or wrong assumptions. Unfortunately, policies sometimes fail due to financial or power interest of specific oligarchic groups, which are part of the dynamic network. In *Short Circuiting Policy*,[40] Leah Stokes examines clean energy policies in the US and explores why many states are not on track to meet the requested adjustments against the climate crisis. One of the conclusions of Stokes' work is that the role of interest groups in shaping clean energy and climate policies is pronounced. She identified the battle between different interest groups and how their influence can hinder or support the development of effective policies.

Environment is the most recent battlefield of interest groups. However, in the past and even now, some interest groups even hinder poverty reduction around the world. Wealthy individuals or corporations may resist redistributive policies or reforms that could reduce wealth inequality. They may use their influence to protect their own interests and block measures that could potentially reduce poverty. Industries involved in extracting and exploiting natural resources, such as mining or oil industries, can hinder poverty reduction. These industries may not adequately benefit the local communities or may cause environmental damage that disproportionately affects the poor. Even powerful landowners and landlords who control large portions of land can hinder poverty reduction efforts, especially in agrarian societies. They may resist land reforms or policies that aim to provide land access or tenure security to the poor. It has also been reported that in some countries, such as Russia,[41] some interest groups might play dirty tricks against competitors also taking advantage of political relationships. This ultimately impacts healthy competition, especially limiting small and innovative companies.

Counterbalancing this is not trivial, as politics and large enterprises have tighter links than private citizens or young startups, and they influence each other. Independently, whether we are policy makers, activists, or entrepreneurs, we need a system thinking approach considering these invisible characters. We cannot design a policy focusing only on the target population. We have multiple actors, different types of stakeholders (including interest groups), and the connections between the parts of the system area are as important as the parts. The theory of systems thinking in health, as described by Don de Savigny, emphasizes an approach to problem solving that recognizes the complex and dynamic nature of systems. According to the theory, systems thinking acknowledges that systems are constantly changing and are influenced by their historical context.[42] This is particularly important when we might have parts of the system opposing useful programs.

In summary, remember that people often act irrationally; or better, their rationale might not be what we think and certain parts of the system might have completely different interests than our goal, therefore working against the policy.

Energy Dome: From Cleantech Startup to Commercial Success

Energy Dome is an energy storage startup founded in 2020, headquartered in Milan, Italy. They aim at developing innovative technologies to store renewable energy in liquid air batteries. The company was cofounded by Claudio Spadacini, Dario Rizzi, and Francesco Oppici.[43]

The innovation

- Energy Dome's carbon dioxide (CO_2) battery technology repurposes CO_2 as a resource to store affordable clean energy and provide renewable baseload power on demand.

- The special battery operates completely emissions-free and can utilize low-grade heat to recharge.

Challenges faced

- As a new startup, raising substantial capital was difficult initially before proving the technology. The initial seed money was given by the founders themselves.

- Educating customers and the energy industry on the benefits of long-duration energy storage and the technology took concerted marketing efforts.

- Scaling up operations and manufacturing the batteries from prototype to commercial scale required overcoming engineering hurdles.

- Italian laws and fees are not supportive to startups. Even considering new policies, costs of incorporation and other taxes are approximatively ten times the costs of opening a company in Poland or Malta,[44] which are also EU countries.

Business model and success factors

- Winning grant funding from the European Commission helped accelerate research and development. This validation helped attract VC investors.

- Partnerships with energy companies like Enel Green Power were established, and this allowed real-world demonstration of the technology's capabilities. Indeed, those pilot projects successfully showcased the solution.

- The experienced founding team, with a strong background in energy, thermal systems, and engineering, provided credibility.

- Expanding operations beyond Italy to the Middle East and United States opened up larger markets.

Impact

Energy Dome's innovation addresses climate change by decarbonizing electricity through its technology. This has a series of positive benefits to society, addressing the current environmental crisis directly (turn to the last chapter for more details).

Key takeaways

- After two years, Energy Dome achieved commercial success. The company has numerous contracts for CO_2 battery installations, and raised over EUR€50 million in funding. Continued global expansion and more partnerships with utilities promise further success. Italy can be seen as both Arizona and

Mexico in the previous chapter: high taxes and entry expenses, though access to research EU grants, talents from universities, and established strong companies allowing collaboration are present (Enel in this case).

- The power distance and culture are difficult to quantify, as the general culture is uncertainty avoidant, but at the same time with "masculinity issues," leading to risk seeking and betting behavior also in business.[45] Uncertainty avoidance is generally a negative trait, while masculinity is positive. In summary, it is like a zoo, it is highly circumstantial.

- This case study depicts a situation of relatively hostile systems from the point of view of the government and institutions, but with communities and human resources favoring business.

Summary

It is time to put the pieces together before we introduce the heroes of this book. The main culprit of a country or a context staying in poverty is their government or local institutions. Fixing this with foreign aid or policies is not easy, as many aspects can also be related to behavioral and psychological aspects.

What is left when your government fails? You. You are the only hope. You can start a revolution from nothing. You are the one you were waiting for. Let me help you with this in the next chapter. Development is not necessarily confined to governments or institutions.

THREE

Mastering Adversity Through Ideas

Every year, poverty kills millions of people.[46] It is so unfortunate that we have yet to find an effective solution to this devastating problem. Even if we are not considering the context of extreme poverty, many places around the world are stuck in a stagnating, non-evolving society. As stated in the previous chapter, critical theories against foreign aid have pointed out that flooding aid into a country might do more harm than good in solving the problem. It is necessary to decentralize development strategies to include local communities in decision-making, recognize urgent local needs, and harness priceless local capabilities. Additionally, it calls for political representation, high levels of civic involvement, and good standards of literacy to be able to participate in a wide variety of decisions on development alternatives.

Reduction of disparity in education, gender difference, import–export, peace, and stability have also shown to bear a huge impact.[47] Yet, it might not be enough to create the spark that radically changes an underserved area into a booming economy. In previous chapters, we discussed known theories related to factors that can hamper development, and gave examples from literature on issues that have to be taken into account. In this chapter, we move into the proactive side of what can be done.

Who are the actors with more skin in the game that need to—and ultimately do—really understand poor people's lives? You: the activists, NGO members, or entrepreneurs reading this book. You: the young scientists with ideas, willing to translate them in the world, not just write them in a scientific paper.

Achieving prosperity

When the right solutions do not come from the top, they have to come from the bottom. Practically, this means civil society, local movements, and entrepreneurs, as we are looking for the bottom beyond local decentralized institutions. Obviously, each country in the long term has to regulate and make formal policies to promote wealth and manage all socio-political circumstances, especially to prevent private companies from not paying taxes, or other unethical behavior. In the case of lack of successful steps to increase wealth in a region or country, the private sector must provide the initial spark.

Disruptive innovation has been the core work of Professor Clayton Christensen during his employment at Harvard University.[48] Briefly, "disruption" describes a process whereby a company with few resources is able to successfully challenge established incumbent businesses. Reframing poverty as a market innovation issue, the late works of Christensen and colleagues proposed an entrepreneur-centric approach against poverty, where the entrepreneur, during his fights to establish a business through innovation or disruption, is addressing poverty-related issues.[49]

Indeed, there is a lot of evidence that prosperity begins when there are investments in market-creating innovation. This is ascribable to entrepreneurs who frequently act as catalysts for creating long-term economic development. Market-creating innovation not only generates jobs and profits; it can also change the culture of a society. For instance, to set up a factory in a forsaken corner of Nigeria, one might need to fix the local sewers that the local government never managed to repair. This is obviously going to eat into the budget and it has to be done according to return of investment, otherwise it does not make sense.[50]

Market-creating innovation is often not just about a product or service; it is a whole system that pulls in new infrastructure and regulations. Entrepreneurs are definitely more in contact with populations than abstract policies and foreign aid. Indeed, societal transformation driven by the needs of the entrepreneur can be seen as a pull mechanism for development, while push approaches attempt to foster a country's development by promoting resources. Push approaches are high level and initiated by institutions or government, lacking the close contact with people. They also lack the "failure is not an option" mindset of entrepreneurs. Moreover, being based as a business also lays the foundation of sustainability as the revenues themselves have to sustain the future company, rather than further donations or grants.

Additionally there are examples of businesses driving the economy of entire countries, like the example of Samsung in South Korea.[51] Sub-Saharan Africa has been one of the economic Cinderellas of our planet, nevertheless recent advancements in communication and information technology led to a series of successful innovations and promising startups. The continent is now booming thanks to local accelerator programs and VC investors.

Citing a few examples, Lami[52] is a Kenyan startup addressing the digital insurance market across the whole African continent. After the rise of phone-money, insurance is now the most promising business in Africa, Latin America, and South Asia. Edukoya is a Nigerian startup operating in the ed-tech context.[53] They act as connectors between African students and teachers for on-demand real-time online learning. mPharma is a medtech startup from Ghana, focused on creating a digital network of pharmacies across Africa.[54]

Most of these companies rely on IT infrastructure, and subsequently have increased the demand and offer to have them locally. Even though they have not built the IT infrastructure directly, they have pushed the system to augment them, with positive side effects unrelated to them. Indeed, in restaurants, people are now placing online food orders, and logistics and educational sectors are compelled to implement digital solutions to stay up with demand, meet new expectations, and retain consumers. These companies are increasing demand for data centers by storing, exchanging, and transferring data in a smooth manner to prevent disruptions in their supply chains.

MoringaConnect

One of the tourist attractions in Ghana is the Kakum National Park near Cape Coast, where you can walk on a canopy path full of moringa trees. I visited in 2012 and even had the experience of sleeping in a treehouse inside the national park, with monkeys jumping on the roof in the middle of the night because of the rain, a 500-star hotel. The guide, a young local boy sleeping with us in the treehouse, introduced me to the mighty moringa tree—a miracle tree that can be used for everything. The leaves have antioxidant nutrients that can feed you for days, you can make ointments for your skin, and even clean your teeth with the bark. To be honest, I never used the bark as a toothbrush or satisfied my appetite with those leaves, and I thought this young guide was crazy, until I heard of MoringaConnect and TrueMoringa a few years later; an example of social entrepreneurship that I want to mention.

MoringaConnect is a platform created by Kwami Williams and Emily Cunningham that connects over 2,500 small farmers in Ghana to the more global Indian market.[55] They cover the interaction between farmers and distributions abroad. Kwami Williams is a Massachusetts Institute of Technology (MIT) graduate aerospace engineer, who after working for NASA decided to move back to Ghana to start a business related to moringa. Emily Cunningham was already involved in microcredit and poverty alleviation programs. They were also part of the D-Lab program. They created a line of cosmetics based on moringa seeds, which are more effective for skin treatment than jojoba or argan oil, turning a miracle tree into a miracle business.

The main innovation was not creating a product (the cosmetic moringa seed-based one), or using the few trees the founders had in their test land, but they created an entire ecosystem. They needed to involve other farmers, training them to be part of their business.

They had to create an integrated supply chain, connecting the dots between the farmers. Training the farmers was not trivial; it included further agricultural training. Nevertheless, they engaged with 2,300 farmers, and the side effect was also pushing further forestation. Obviously, the basis was to create a sustainable business, but in doing so they increased local agricultural education, which can also be used by local farmers for other purposes, and planted numerous trees. They also gave seeds and fertilizer, and there are solar-powered systems on the way to avoid drought periods using sustainable energy.

Williams' and Cunningham's original plan was to just sell machinery to harvest and process moringa. Nonetheless, this was a bad market fit. They had to improve the farming ecosystem overall. These are the positive side effects that social entrepreneurship, or even traditional entrepreneurship, created on the way to a sustainable business. This is the prosperity paradox created by entrepreneurs, not by humanitarian organizations.

The MoringaConnect story sounds like a nice one, but indeed it contains all elements for a successful business that we can reproduce. Obviously, about 60% of new successful and sustainable businesses are specific, but we can focus on the remaining 40% that can be crafted, for which we have models and known approaches.

(Bio)design thinking

It crept in slowly at first, just a few concerning reports here and there, whispers of a mysterious new illness emerging overseas in China. Then, on 30 January 2020, the World Health Organization declared the coronavirus outbreak a "pandemic."[56] All of a sudden, we were living in an unprepared world of constant contrasting news and strange social rules. We needed rapid tests to validate the presence of the virus, we needed a vaccine, among other things. The size of the epidemic put pressure on us to find solutions. In this case, the needs were relatively clear. Luckily, in 2023 the emergency was (hopefully) over—or at least we have enough tools to fight back. On the other hand, in our society there are probably other needs that are ignored by scientists, policy makers, and entrepreneurs, which do exist if you look carefully.

Technology innovators in both business and academia often follow a "technology push" strategy: a technology or approach is discovered, and it is the new "hammer" used for all nails. They go searching for applications in different domains or their familiar domain (eg oncology or neuroimaging). This approach is especially common in biotech and pharmaceutical development, where scientific discoveries, such as a new mathematical model, a new molecule, or a new deep-learning architecture, ultimately lead to the creation of a new health biomarker.

It is indisputable that we have reached many goals with this mindset, but the distinctive characteristic of (medical) technology is that it's almost always possible to start with important unmet needs and then invent a technology that will help solve them. This need-driven approach is not well understood or practiced by either industry or academia. Unfortunately, this often leads to fancy innovative products and services that nobody wants.

The key questions here are:

- How do we find unmet needs?
- Are all unmet needs the same?

The short answer is: you need to read literature about it and directly ask the users. Not all needs are the same. Finding the vaccine for coronavirus in 2020 did not have the same urgency as optimizing the segmentation of a brain tumor in a magnetic resonance imaging (MRI). Although there might be less competition in the latter case, and ultimately it will be easier to dominate the market. Things are not white or black; you have to consider the overall picture.

Elements of unmet medical needs can be found in literature. Often, scientific papers mention limitations of proposed technologies in their discussion or conclusion sections, so we can find unsolved issues and then carry on with our creativity, but this is not the only way. There are blueprints to find unmet needs methodically. Assuming we do not believe in magic "eureka" moments and we focus on addressing needs, there are existing frameworks like the Stanford Biodesign method,[57] or the Test Evaluation Working Group of the European Federation of Clinical Chemistry and Laboratory Medicine (EFLM TE-WG) checklist,[58] which can be used daily, looking for innovation.

Generally, unmet needs should be mostly related to pressing patient and societal needs. We can take a closer look at the Venn diagram below, inspired by the figure in Vreman et al.[59] A need is more relevant if it concerns a large proportion of a population, for example looking at cardiovascular disease rather than a rare genetic disease. It is better if the need is also urgent or involves severe diseases, eg having a fast testing protocol for the coronavirus during the outbreak does not have the same urgency as designing a shuttle for Mars—or at least it should not. With this I do not want to minimize the value of research on rare diseases, but to highlight that at societal level, unfortunately they are less urgent compared to global outbreaks or similar circumstances.

We need to consider the current available solutions, as what we will propose might be comparable to these, or indeed worse than them and therefore not addressing the need in the end. Lastly, we need to know whether the technology is feasible, or at least achievable, through research and development within a reasonable amount of time.

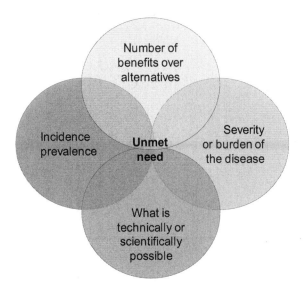

Elements of unmet medical needs found in definitions and possible ways to measure them (adapted from Vreman et al. 2019)

With those considerations in mind, let's delve into existing models for (bio)design thinking. The Stanford Biodesign method[60] comprises the following steps:

- **The "Identify" phase** is about finding relevant unmet needs from literature, observing, and asking. We need to observe real people and real-life situations. When we ask questions, we need to listen to the answers without assuming we have already the solution.

- **The "Invent" phase** refers to the brainstorming process undertaken by experts, proposing many potential solutions. Then, ideas are organized objectively and compared against key criteria to satisfy the needs. Now, prototypes are built in a rapid "think-build-rethink" sequence.

- **The "Implement" phase** is related to topics discussed later in this book, such as developing a strategy or writing a business plan. In the end, it is like a survival of the fittest where the survival device / model / prototype might reach actual patients and will not be just a scientific paper or patent. In the implement phase, we proceed in prototyping and testing the technology, developing the approach to patenting, and regulatory approval.

Machine learning, quantum computing, and whatever we have not thought about yet goes into the "invent" or "implement" steps, rather than the starting point, so they are used *after* the need has been identified, not before.

In practice, the critical step is the identification of needs. As Buddhists and children do, we should observe the problem with a beginner's mind, following the users closely and looking for clues, without assuming we already know the answers. The core strategy in exploring needs is to dive into the clinical environment, looking for suboptimal patient outcomes, recurring complications, frustrations on the part of care providers, or other signs of problems in care delivery.

In today's healthcare environment, innovators should actively look for opportunities to improve on value—that is, focusing on the cost as well as the outcome of care. The work is substantially done by observing, discussing, and looking at healthcare workers. They are not going to easily tell what their needs are that should be improved. We should remember the saying from Henry Ford: "If I had asked my customers what they wanted, they would have said a faster horse." In practical terms, we need to talk to physicians, patients, and other potential end users to understand their pain. An ideal situation is to have multiple identified needs and then choose the most meaningful by validating these needs with the stakeholders.

The implementation step can be devised in many ways, and it generally depends on which strategy we choose. Depending on the point of view we prefer, many aspects can change a lot. According to the Stanford Biodesign recommendations, a non-exhaustive list of strategies can be:[61]

- Intellectual property-based – what can be patented and what can be protected in other ways, for example, having a network or a Food and Drug Administration (FDA) approval

- Fostered by research and development – which expertise and technologies can we exploit?

- Focused on clinical aspects

- Constrained by regulatory issues

- Based on marketing

- Limited by sales and distribution circumstances

A relevant aspect of biodesign thinking is choosing a strategic focus. This involves firstly deciding on the values or what the organization looking for innovation wants to accomplish. Secondly, accurately determining whatever abilities the innovator or business has (or does not possess) that will have an impact on their capacity to achieve those objectives. Last but not least, converting these insights into standards that can be applied to impartially assess opportunities and choose which issues or priority areas to pursue. As an alternative to the Stanford model, the EFLM TE-WG has developed a comprehensive checklist for the evaluation of analytical methods used in laboratory medicine.

This checklist serves as a guide, evaluating and verifying novel analytical methods and instruments. Laboratory experts should adhere to a consistent and structured process. The checklist is a clinically driven method to formalize the role and vision of a technology. Unmet needs are often relatively vaguely defined and the checklist aims at reducing this vagueness. The TE-WG method follows four steps and four key-domains. The four steps are:

1. Analyzing literature

2. Carrying out meetings about strategy

3. Receiving feedback from end users

4. Performing testing and improvement utilizing case studies

These four steps then further comprise fourteen questions, which form the actual checklist.[62] These questions include:

- What is the target group?

- What are the limitations of the current practice?

- Could the problem be solved by optimizing current practice?

- How do the new solution outcomes compare to those defined previously?

- Under what conditions would the new biomarker be feasible?

Models and checklists are valuable tools to assist the work of scientists, stakeholders, and innovators involved in the discovery or implementation of new biomarkers and testing strategies. The use of these approaches is encouraged to shift from the technology center view to the unmet need view (where actually we should say patient- or customer-centric view). In the next section, I list a series of less formal ideas to identify potential unmet needs.

How to find ideas

The most common way large companies identify new ideas is simply monitoring what is going on in the academic world, or even just listening to pitches of startups trying to be acquired.[63] If you ask the founders of successful companies how they found the idea at the basis of their venture, they will tell you something along the lines of: "I have noticed this issue, and I knew how to address it...." Everything starts with a problem, and we need to ask: "What is the problem?" Firstly, "Why do we want to be an activist, entrepreneur, scientist, etc" and secondly, "What is the problem we want to address?" As mentioned in the previous section, having a solution looking for a problem might not be the winning strategy. Instead of romanticizing "eureka" moments people might have in the shower, in this section I listed a series of strategies we can all follow to find problems people might have. These are relatively anecdotal and I do not have scientific evidence or statistics on one strategy being more productive than others; some are reported in various texts on design thinking, though.[64] I hope they will be of great inspiration.

As a first step, I would propose you spend at least ten days annotating every problem you see in the real world. We must first identify a pressing issue before formulating a "problem statement" and then considering potential solutions. A way to find a pressing issue could be to note every difficulty we observe people facing. A problem might arise in our place of employment, at home, or even on the street. Once a lengthy list of issues has been compiled, the following step is to evaluate it and draw some judgments to see if there are any potential marketable solutions. From all these challenges we should see if we can devise any possible solutions that can be monetized. The definition of the value proposition will follow naturally as a result.

It is important to continue paying attention to this for more than just one day. A long period of study would be advantageous because difficulties do not always surface in a single day. It would make more sense to follow and study the ideal client persona and discover which obstacles he or she faces over a long enough period of time if we are interested in a certain niche. For instance, if you are an engineer working in medical technology, you should observe doctors, nurses, and technicians for at least ten days.

If you have a specific ideal customer persona in mind, ask them. Asking people directly about their pain during the day might be a simple fix, rather than seeking problems. This, however, requires that the person being interviewed already has all the answers. Most likely, this is not the case. Some people will find it easy to articulate their issues but others may be less eager to acknowledge difficulties or offer suggested remedies. Straightforward questions like: "What solution might be useful to you?" can often lead to anywhere.

There are several frameworks related to gamification or based on empathy that can be used. Deep conversations that focus on various facets of the prospective clients' lives are vital to have.

Empathy maps are visual canvases where one should annotate what the ideal customer persona says, thinks, feels, and does.[65] By recording this, they serve as an attempt to gain insight into the target consumers' minds. The customers' gains and pain points are two more crucial components of empathy maps. Any annoyances, challenges, or dangers encountered on their path are referred to as pain points. Similarly, gains need to be listed as those represent the advantages and value that a consumer hopes to get from a hypothetical innovation. Teams can gain a greater understanding of user motivation by identifying these two components. As team members conduct conversations about users, sticky notes are added throughout the various quadrants as part of the highly collaborative empathy mapping process. As more customer insights are gleaned from research and testing, the map expands over time. An effective empathy map should visually convey the main ideas of the target user's point of view. More human-centered products that better meet client needs result from this approach.

Quoting Hamilton Helmer, who introduced the term "counter-positioning":[66] "A newcomer adopts a new, superior business model which the incumbent does not mimic due to anticipated damage to their existing business." Practically, you have to identify a weak point in a successful business, eg a highly downloaded app with a poor rating. If people use them it means there is a demand, but they are not fulfilling the needs totally. A common example was the renting system of Craigslist and the subsequent superior model of Airbnb for housing.[67]

Similarly, sometimes technological shifts lead to innovative solutions that can fulfill better solutions for existing challenges. Artificial intelligence, drones, augmented reality, quantum computing—aside from being buzzwords, these new technologies have opened the door to new business models or better solutions to the demands of the market. However, often novel technologies complicate easy solutions. Entrepreneurs need to be cautious while trying to innovate with technology. How many times have you seen brilliant ideas fail, simply because they were "ahead of their time?" Or perhaps certain trends had no lasting benefits. Do you remember the metaverse? Nevertheless, it is beneficial most of the time to keep an eye out for changes in technology, and the opportunities they bring are essential for technological innovation. For instance, Netflix only started to turn a profit after worldwide internet and mobile broadband speeds were sufficient for high-definition streaming, while Blockbuster was still focused on the physical video-rental model.[68] Now that computers are powerful enough to train and run sophisticated machine-learning models, artificial intelligence is becoming quite widespread.

Similar algorithms already existed twenty to thirty years ago, but it was unimaginable to use them in daily practice due to the lack of infrastructure.

People complain and search for solutions on platforms and forums online (eg Reddit, LinkedIn, Twitter, and Stack Overflow). Here, we can observe the ideal customer persona rants without us interviewing them. Many prosperous businesses look for problems that already exist among their target clients before selecting a new one to tackle. Once you have discovered a problem that is either unsolved or has poor answers, you may step in with a product that appeals to that audience. Go and read what a community is complaining about. You can tap into forums and social media channels and understand what motivates the specific groups that are active on them.

Another opportunity for business owners would be to look into failed projects to see whether they were just "ahead of their time." If so, it's time to take another look at the idea. The best example of this is in games. Nintendo is a typically successful corporation, but it made a disastrous error in 1995 when it introduced the "Virtual Boy" virtual reality device. It sold poorly and was quickly taken off the market because people did not fully grasp what virtual reality was.[69] Just fast-forward a couple of decades and virtual reality is one of the most promising markets.

Creative capacity building

Design thinking and other aforementioned strategies are well-known processes used by companies in the "northern hemisphere." In low-resource settings, we often use "creative capacity building" (CCB), a term introduced by several educators but brought to popularity by the D-Lab at the MIT, referring to methodologies promoting community-driven innovation, giving community members a platform to create answers to the problems they confront.[70] For MIT D-Lab, "community" often refers to rural communities in low-income countries. Nevertheless, the principles of design thinking and CCB are the same in high- and middle-income countries where a group of individuals is seeking innovation.

Twende, a Tanzania-based NGO, deals with the innovation of technologies to solve community challenges.[71] They run programs from one day to eight weeks that encourage creativity and innovative thinking, with the emblematic slogan, "Building a generation of problem-solvers." They also provide a makerspace in North Tanzania, and support and mentorship after the training program. For D-Lab, Twende, and other organizations offering courses on CCB, design thinking is not just for designers or engineers. CCB is for everybody who's trying to find a solution. It is a model that fosters creativity, problem solving, and entrepreneurship in all types of committees.

Having this open mindset is the first step. A radically inclusive approach to collaborative design needs to be achieved to firstly change the culture of people. Programs can also be taught to people with no formal education, and then adapted to them. These programs are not particularly focused on giving a person a single technology, even if knowledge is critical, as we will discuss in the next chapter. The important aspect here is to empower people with a process that they can use again and again to solve a problem, to see themselves as somebody who can find the answers by working out challenges. We might be reminded of the old saying: "Give a man a fish, and you feed him for a day. Teach a man to fish, and you feed him for a lifetime." Giving a CCB workshop is more like, "Don't stop until everyone is fishing, and what do you do when the lake dries and you cannot fish anymore?"

More specifically, CCB workshops focus on community-led livelihood, encouraging people to make and use technologies that generate income, improve health and safety, or save labor and time. In summary, to achieve prosperity in low-resource settings, a new level of capacity building should be implemented, similar to the behavior on the 1990s TV series *MacGyver*. If some readers do not know, *MacGyver* was a TV series about an individual ally to social and environmental causes who gets involved in complicated circumstances.[72] He had a remarkable talent for repurposing commonplace items from his immediate environment to address issues. The most used tool was a Swiss army knife. In some episodes he was portrayed as able to create complicated tools with duct tape, paper clips, and knowledge of physics and chemistry. He represents innovation, invention, and resourcefulness in all cultures. Despite the obvious cinematographic drama, and scientifically inaccurate outcomes in the TV series, we can learn a lot from it. MacGyver is able to improvise with his available tools. He creates something given the time constraints. He uses each nook and cranny of his knowledge and puts it into practice. Entrepreneurs should act similarly. They need to create a product or service with the available resources, and to consider costs and impact. You cannot spend USD\$1,000 to use a medtech expensive electrophoresis chamber; you need to redesign it from acrylic slabs for USD\$5, as this is possible. The process is the same if we build something complicated using cloud computing, quantum devices, and fintech. The mental process is identical, though obviously more knowledge is required.

A typical day of CCB training comprises the following steps:[73]

- Participants introduce themselves and what they have been doing

- Motivation and inspiration is given to the participants

- Introduction of problem solving as a game

- Explaining the design cycle to participants

- Discussion of possible projects

- Transition to skill building

- Project selection

These CCB training steps have the ultimate goal to promote creativity, and to push people seeing new uses of existing tools to solve socio-economic issues. An example of this process can be to see bottle lids as tools to extract seeds or corns, or novel methods of e-learning with curricula focused on young gifted girls in rural areas. Some roleplay has to be included to avoid boredom.

According to the 2020 report on the impact of CCB of local innovators and communities on income, welfare, and attitudes in Uganda,[74] attendance at CCB training doubled the number of economic activities for both long and short workshop CCB beneficiaries. CCB technologies also enhanced equality in the division of labor for agricultural activities, giving women capacity to harvest fruits and men capacity to participate in seed-cleaning activities. CCB training also enhanced the capacity of trainees to fix broken tools. CCB programs are often focused on low-resource settings. I would argue that this kind of thinking should also be used to take advantage of modern technologies as quantum computing and cloud solutions to create high-tech innovation, even if starting with low resources.

Summary

In this chapter we delved into our bottom-up approach. We highlighted that when governments and institutions do not provide improvements for our society, we need to take action. The first step is to have a problem statement, to find an issue and related ideas or solutions. This can be achieved in different ways, such as observing people, discussing with customers, or exploring literature. Particular creative approaches have to be taken when we deal with low-income countries. Through CCB we can look for solutions given financial constraints or limited resources, in the same way as the movie hero MacGyver. Go out into the real world, observe people and their challenges, and find a possible solution.

The next part comprises the steps you need to translate these ideas into the real world.

PART TWO
FROM IDEA TO REALITY

Congratulations! If proper investigations have been carried out, a suitable problem statement has now been defined with possible related innovative solutions. Now it is time to translate this idea into reality—in academia, we call it "technology transfer."

This part of the book is focused on a series of practical aspects that have to be considered, to transfer the idea from our minds or our scientific paper into a policy or a business.

FOUR
Technology Transfer

This chapter is pure practice and is aimed at anybody in this planet, while the next chapter focuses explicitly on low-resource settings.

Now that you have an idea, it is time to mingle in the community to get further input. You need to find cofounders; you need to decide on your initial strategy and how you protect yourself and your idea. Even if you open source and have no patent, you need a minimum of leverage to be chosen by investors and survive.

Initial steps for activists and entrepreneurs

Just having a problem statement and an innovation to address will not be enough; one needs to have a strategy and a series of actionable steps. Rob Hopkins is an environmental activist and deep thinker who wrote several books on this topic. He is the founder and leading figure of the Transition Movement. In *The Transition Companion* he proposed a series of steps to create a successful movement.[75] The model is highly focused on environmental issues for non-profit organizations.

Here I report an adapted to-do list, written in a more general manner, skipping steps specific to environmental actions from Hopkins' tools of transition:

1. Stand up to speak (understanding and measurement)

2. Transition training (visioning, creativity/ imagination)

3. Create awareness (running meetings and forming working groups)

4. Have a legal entity (register your association or company, build partnerships)

5. Speak with the press

6. Find some funding for the organization

7. Create a street-by-street behavioral change

8. Have a constant presence in the media

9. Work with local businesses

10. Build a bridge to local institutions to create suitable policies

The initial step is to create a minimal critical mass gathering of people. This can happen through some public speaking events or contexts where a specific subculture meets. The role of storytelling is now crucial. Once a group of people is engaged, a vision challenging the current status quo has to be defined. Given goals and vision, a legal entity must be established, and this is highly dependent on the country of foundation.

The next steps are financing and drawing attention. Financing can be given through donations or grants. Grants or other forms of funding obtained by associations or groups of people are generally not as pronounced as the financing available to governments or large institutions, but the process is the same. Drawing attention is critical, both in terms of being seen by mass media such as national magazines, and also grass-roots activities such as discussions with laymen in the street.

To deepen effectiveness, developing a good relationship with the local authority will be vital. Local councilors and stakeholders are just people. They have to feel part of the process and it is important that they are invited to events such as film screenings as guests of honor and invited to speak. Social media is also vital, from X (formerly Twitter) and Instagram to personal blogs. It is difficult to know when, but slowly the organization will scale up and ultimately will be able to be seen as a local authority, and at that point even invited into the design of policies for transitions.

Hopkins' texts are full of examples of small businesses or communities gaining success in Ireland following his steps. I want to reiterate these steps as they are relevant for any changemaker. The upcoming chapters are not specific to social entrepreneurship, but are a guided way to achieve prosperity through any kind of entrepreneurship. The perspective is that all entrepreneurs are heroes, assuming they act ethically.

In the rest of this chapter, I would like to guide you through a list of steps more focused on startups I made:

1. Find cofounders

2. Define how you protect yourself from competition

3. Have a go-to-market strategy

4. Find your initial customers

5. Launch as soon as possible and get feedback

If you have all these steps in place, when you talk to investors you will already have most of the answers. Those steps are not exhaustive, just the first I suggest that you address.

In the next chapter, I will focus on more specific aspects for the Global South or low-resource settings, while Chapter 6 discusses other nuts and bolts related to certification, business models, and growth. Before we delve into those steps, it is good to remind ourselves that a social innovation or new product requires some changes in our society or in the mind of a customer, and this might be less straightforward than people think.

Barriers to change

The fact we like to talk about "change" often is actually because it's not easy. Change is difficult; sometimes the hurdles are overwhelming. In *Change*,[76] Professor Damon Centola from the University of Pennsylvania summarized the barriers to change in four categories: coordination, credibility, legitimacy, and excitement.

Coordination emphasizes that certain innovations make sense when many people use them simultaneously, such as with Facebook, Skype, and M-PESA. To convince skeptical people to adopt changes, they need to see other people using them, and therefore they can interact with them—the more the better. Credibility is about gaining trust through social proof, as people tend to be wary of new things until they see others adopting them without issues. We wait to see whether a vaccine has crazy side effects before having it. Legitimacy is also tied to social acceptance, ensuring a behavior aligns with societal norms, like dressing in a specific way or having certain behaviors. Excitement stresses that innovations need to connect with emotional contexts, as seen with X's role in the #blacklivesmatter movement.

A common element to overcoming barriers and being accepted is social proof of an innovation or social aspect. Spreading news and scientific reports about the environment with the subsequent need of using solar panels is not effective to move people toward this kind of social change, but if you see all your neighbors with a solar panel on their roofs you will immediately buy one. Regrettably, social proofs are more effective than scientific divulgation and rational argumentations.[77] Expecting the "fear of missing out" appears to help: if you see your neighbor with a solar panel, you also want it.

It's hard enough to change our own habits, so changing an entire culture is even harder. Yet, history shows that it is possible. Later in this chapter, we will consider some approaches that can be beneficial in this.

How to find cofounders

We do not go far alone. Except in special cases, ventures that succeed need to have two or three main founders. If you have an idea, you need partners complementing you. It is important that you are aligned with vision and that you can work together, even remotely, for as long as it works. For NGOs, foundations, and other types of organizations, it seems less critical, but it is the same; you need a legal representative, a president, and a treasurer. These can rarely be the same person. Having cofounders in a startup or partners in a business is like a love relationship, and not just at the beginning when you find each other.

Moreover, it is important to involve people who can handle stress and have a similar level of motivation. Like in a relationship, someone might be looking for fun and another might be looking to get married, have kids, etc. It is the same in business; some people already have a job and would like to do something on the side (and they think thirty minutes per week will be enough), and other people are ready to work twenty-five hours a day on an idea, and even sleep in their car if things get tough, as long as they have a successful startup.

Indeed, it is not just finding people but keeping them. There will be many moments when the startup or business will be like a rocking boat, as any marriage is, so it is better to find people who can endure the same level of stress as you. A certain level of trust is needed.

Now that you have been warned, where do you find partners or cofounders? Like with relationships, start with people you already know in your existing social circle: friends, colleagues, schoolmates.

In the majority of cases, to all startups I asked in my life where the founders met, the answer has been one of the above cases. In my experience, "former colleagues" was the most common answer. However, social circles might be limited. Do not fall into the trap of creating a business with your close circle because those are the only people you know; you might end up in the misaligned scenarios I mentioned in the previous section. Going through your social media contacts and even posting about this need on Facebook, X, LinkedIn, Reddit, etc will be the first step. Just be aware who you are getting with; you do not marry the first guy or girl you matched with on Tinder, or do you?

An alternative to social media are platforms or websites for founders where you can find people with similar mindset. At the time of writing, I recommend the following:

- **Y Combinator**, the world's largest startup accelerator, has a free Co-Founder Matching program.[78]

- **CoFoundersLab** is a community of 400,000 members. They also have a paid membership plan, including access to courses and learning material to upskill your project management, and more control in messaging potential cofounders.[79]

- **Indie Hackers** is a nerdy community, strongly oriented to the IT sector.[80]

- **Founders List** is an open platform for founders to connect and launch ideas and products. It is clearly stated in the splash page that it is meant for finding cofounders.[81]

- **F6S** connects four million founders and startups to funding, jobs, and free hosting deals.[82]

- **Founders DAO** is a community of investors and startuppers. You can post about the fact you are looking for cofounders.[83]

- **Trends.vc** has a large network.[84]

...and many more probably exist. Apart from what the internet can offer, there are other old-school ways. Going to meetups, conferences, or even startup pitches are good opportunities.

What do you do if you live in the Global South (southern Asia, sub-Saharan Africa, or Latin America)? The issue might be that the platforms I previously mentioned are used more by Europeans or Americans. It is better to consider other options if you want a partner or cofounder living in your same country.

I hope you are not introvert, because this is the hard truth: you need to go to meetings, events, and conferences, and approach people. Those can be hackathons, for example the SPARK-Brain Tumor Segmentation Challenge,[85] the Consortium for Advancement of MRI education and research in Africa (CAMERA),[86] or the Africa Open Science Hardware summit.[87] Or you could physically go to coworking spaces or physical hubs with a community of people, such as the Kumasi Hive[88] in Ghana (a list, my fellow sub-Saharan friends, is given in the Further Reading section). It does not necessarily have to be a fixed place; it can be a meetup hosted in a different place each time.

Communities are not just places to find cofounders. Every innovator should be immersed in physical spaces for collaboration. The CCB approach described in the previous chapter focuses on enabling all members of the community—including the poorest and most disadvantaged—to develop the necessary skills and capabilities to participate in entrepreneurial activities. This includes providing training, education, and mentorship programs that empower individuals to start and sustain their own businesses. By equipping community members with the necessary tools and knowledge, CCB initiatives contribute to the overall development and economic empowerment of the community. This is valid for low-income countries and also for high-income countries.

A policy maker should establish coworking spaces or innovation hubs where entrepreneurs can work, share resources, and collaborate—or at least create the opportunities for them to raise ideas. These spaces can also provide access to tools, equipment, and facilities that entrepreneurs may not have on their own. Collaborative spaces are the first places where an innovator, entrepreneur, or activist can get cheap, informal feedback, hear about funding opportunities, and access other relevant information.

Collaborative spaces can be physical coworking spaces or virtual platforms that bring together entrepreneurs from diverse backgrounds. Through shared resources, knowledge exchange, and networking opportunities, collaborative spaces help entrepreneurs overcome financial limitations and access valuable support networks. A community is not a virtual or physical space, it can be found in interactions. Entrepreneurs are advised to actively seek out such spaces within their communities or leverage digital platforms to connect with like-minded individuals. If you live in a remote suburb in Bangladesh, you can start connecting to online communities.

Incubators and accelerators are initiatives designed to support early-stage startups in their growth journey. These programs provide entrepreneurs with access to capital, mentorship, training, and industry connections. Entrepreneurs in low-income countries should actively explore and engage with such programs, as they offer a structured approach to scaling up their ventures and increasing their chances of success.

Patents and other protection

Most universities have technology transfer offices, which are supposed to guide scientists in the creation of startup companies or any other form of commercialization from their research. Their steps include predisclosure, protection, and licensing. Unfortunately, there is a strong focus on intellectual property protection, sometimes without a good practical understanding. Moreover, some people are against patents for good reasons. Indeed, there are other ways, and even if you want to use patents, there are ways to handle them without going bankrupt or acting like a secret agent. If your startup is not stemming from academia you have a little more freedom, but the dilemmas are the same.

Imagine your business success as a castle, with you, your cofounders, and your customers in it. You should have a moat, otherwise anybody can enter it and take over, even overnight. This ingenious use of waterways allows you and your business to withstand several sieges during history, like Archimedes inside the Maniace Castle in Syracuse. If you have some pitching experience, you very often may have heard, "How do you protect yourself?" Competent people will understand if you have "a moat," people reciting this question off the cuff with little practical experience will simply dump you if you do not have a patent. Assuming you met the first ones, they are asking you about your "moat." Let me introduce the concept, then we will review some practical aspects about patents and go into patent-less solutions. An economic moat is a company's protective competitive advantage over rivals. Patents are not the only way, there are several other types of "moats"—I list only six below. Their choice generally depends on the fields of the innovation. On the one hand, the pharma industry is strongly tightened with patents, as drug design is a long process, and therefore we need to define something in the long term. On the other hand, software houses are built in days and they are successful too, so we need something faster.

1. Patents

This is the most common, tormented, and discussed approach. When you have an idea, you can submit detailed documentation to specific offices that will confirm the intellectual property. A patent is an exclusive right granted for an invention. What is an invention depends strongly on the claim we declare to the patent office.

Patents are also geographically limited and the costs are related to the country we are interested in. Geography also matters relating to the definition of what an "invention" is. In Europe, software or data manipulation are hardly patentable, while in the US this is possible.

Despite all the general obsessions about having a patent for everything, patents cost. It costs to find an attorney to support the process, there are maintenance expenses, and it takes time to obtain a patent—on average two to four years. Moreover, patents do not guarantee any kind of protection against copycats on their own; they have to be used by the applicant in case of suing, and often people are experts in finding solutions to swing around patents—it is a legal nightmare. A patent guarantees to investors that you own your innovation, and large companies love to attack each other on this point. A startup should only follow this path if it makes sense to.

Moreover, during the process of obtaining a patent there is supposed to be no disclosure, no public presentation, nor publishing papers, etc. How can a young company proceed with funding, partnership, and so on without disclosure? It is not an easy situation.

Patents can be utility patent, provisional patent, design patent, and plant patent. We do not discuss design and plant patents here because they are a bit out of topic. People usually call on utility patents when thinking about patents.

Let's move onto your best friend: provisional patents! Provisional patents are patent applications that can be used to secure a filing date. They are filed in the United States Patent and Trademark Office (USPTO) – the European Patent Office (EPO) does not allow it – and do not require a formal patent claim. They can be filed informally, without adhering to the strict formatting of non-provisional applications. The best part: they allow you to disclose your innovation in public. A provisional patent expires after twelve months, and then either the patent dies or you file a full utility patent.

Your steps could be:

1. File a provisional patent.

2. Talk to investors, go to conferences, etc.

3. If the idea is worth the time and money, file a utility patent.

Nevertheless, this is not a dogma and, in some cases, other moats are more relevant.

Lastly, while patents are not necessarily the best moats, it is critical to verify that our invention is not violating any previous claims, making sure we have the so-called freedom to operate in the specific country of our interest.

2. Network effect

Many people will agree that network effect is the single most potent moat in practice—especially in the tech space. The more people using a product or service, the better it is. You can copy Facebook's website, but without the people inside Facebook it will have little value.

Economy of scale is highly associated with network effect. Increased numbers of people improve the value of goods or services. If you use advertisements on your platform, you can price the advertisement according to how many users you have in your network. If you are reaching out to investors, you can show the value of your platform by the number of users. There is no need to have a patent (which you could not have in Europe because a web platform cannot be patented at all).

3. Unique dataset

In the deep-learning AI world, having large datasets to train models is a relevant aspect – even more so than the machine-learning architecture itself. Having a unique dataset that competitors will take ages to recreate can be considered a moat. In this way, you indirectly guarantee that you have a unique solution, or at least a specific model trained in a more specific way than the competition.

This is more relevant for AI MedTech solutions rather than pure Software as a Service (SaaS) solutions. In those AI-model-based solutions, training from an exclusive dataset is even more important than the network effect.

4. Branding

Consumers may become attached to their favorite brands. It is like a loose networking effect. People trust a brand because historically they have proven to offer high-quality products or services. Therefore, you pay more for something that other customers believe is of higher value. Often branding is associated to status (eg a Ferrari or a Bulgari bag) or a person or character (you love that rockstar or fictional character associated to a specific company, such as Super Mario).

Generally, branding takes time and is difficult to quantify numerically. Therefore it is not seen by investors to be as strong as patents of reported network effect, unless the brand is so strong that the investors already know about it.

5. Pivotal partnership

Maybe you do not have a big brand on your own. You can join existing well-known brands with a strong contract. Strategic partnerships and contracts with other established brands can indirectly be a moat. If you can have, or can show that your service will provide exclusive collaboration with famous brands, this will represent a secure way to gain customers, and investors may believe you.

6. Certification

In Chapter 5 we will discuss more in-depth details regarding certification, but here we should at least mention what they represent from the point of view of protection. Having certification, such as for medical devices, is costly and time-consuming—if we achieve this. We are definitely in an advantaged position compared to our competitors. Again, this is not as strong as a patent or a network effect but definitely gives some safeguarding, which investors will acknowledge.

Obviously, nothing is forever, for example all the network effect of Myspace has gone right now.[89] Finding a moat is the best available defense that businesses have in hostile and competitive markets, but it is not an absolute guarantee of success. Nevertheless, it allows businesses to enter markets and to be perceived as valuable by investors.

Go-to-market strategy

Early-stage startups often make the common mistake of believing their product is revolutionary, and people will be so impressed by the solution they introduce. Maybe they used some novel technology and it sounds so hot. This is *not* what people outside your little world will think. People do not care what a product does or whether it uses quantum-AI embedded in liquid neurons. Instead, people have their own pain, and they might be interested in something that can alleviate it.

A further complication is the lack of trust. I sometimes hear, "Yes, this is a cool idea, I love it, but I will not buy it." People generally do not trust new things unless they have come through a proper branding campaign, as we just said. Having a cool product or service is just half of the work. It is not enough to have built something and managed to fund it. Half of the job is to convince customers your something is alleviating some of their pain and that they can trust it. We still need to overcome the four barriers to change we mentioned earlier in this chapter. Unfortunately, this might even happen to products or services with a promising product-market fit.

A starting point to answer all these concerns can be to have a go-to-market (GTM) strategy. A GTM strategy is a plan defining the necessary steps to at least acquire initial customers in a new market.[90] Those initial steps should include the following first actions:

- Define the ideal customer profile in the most detailed way.

- Find out what the right price for this ideal customer is.

- Reach out and build trust with ideal customers.

- Convert most of them into effective customers, and measure this.

- In case things do not work as expected, pivot as soon as possible and reiterate.

First, we need to define the ideal customer profile in the most detailed way. Whatever was in your marketing plan, you need to go deeper. The more narrowed and specific the ideal customer for the product-market-fit is, the better life will be afterwards. For example, when writing this, I had in mind a specific category of people: either someone with limited resources—not much money, not many relevant connections, not much experience—yet willing to do something, or a scientist in academia with little understanding of how to move from academia to industry but wanting to create a startup. If we consider the last subgroup, the ideal person is currently enrolled in an MSc or PhD program, finishing it soon, and has some ideas. This means that this person is following specific Reddit channels, Facebook groups, and so on, which I can target. In more general terms, gather information about your target market, competitors, industry trends, and customer preferences. Reach out and build trust with your ideal customers. Once you have found the necessary communication channels related to your ideal customer profile, it is time to test them.

We need to determine the most effective channels to reach your target audience. These could include direct sales, Facebook groups, online marketing, partnerships, distributors, or a combination of channels. Consider factors such as reach, cost, efficiency, and customer preferences. Communicate in these channels and with those ideal customers (eg opening a waiting list splash page and asking the ideal customers to sign up). Now the questions are:

- Does your ideal customer respond to marketing efforts such as magazines, social media, or niche websites?

- Where does your target audience spend most of their time?

We need to convert these ideal customers into real customers, then convert most of these real customers into effective customers, and measure this. Many aspects of this resemble approaches I previously summarized in the section about finding the first customers. The objectives you establish will have a direct impact on whether your GTM plan is successful. You provide the measurements you'll use to gauge your success as you set these goals.

It is crucial to monitor your key performance indicators as your plan develops and to make any necessary adjustments along the way. Common criteria used to gauge a GTM strategy's effectiveness include customer acquisition costs and closing/conversion rates, to be checked either daily, weekly, or monthly. These metrics are used intensively by businesses based on online platforms, such as SaaS companies. Nevertheless, they can be used in most businesses.

If the conversion is poor, it is better not to be stubborn or too attached to the designed strategy (or product). It is time to change something; otherwise, the risk is to end up a complete failure. Once a small, smart change is made, it is time to reiterate the process from the beginning, especially measuring the conversion from people reached into real customers.

In summary, a GTM strategy is a comprehensive plan that guides a company's efforts to introduce and promote its products or services. By considering target audience identification, product positioning, pricing, distribution channels, and promotional activities, a company can effectively reach its customers and grow from there.

How companies get their first hundred clients

With an ideal customer persona in mind and a GTM strategy, we can finally enter the real world. Here I review with you a list of possible target people that can be involved in the first days, also referring to how other companies started.

I asked several startups in the biotech and medtech field how they started. Getting their first customers has been a particularly challenging issue for them. Their customers are not so easy to find as for social media platforms, and considering they deal with health, there is a considerable level of resistance and trust needed. As mentioned by Bartosz Borucki, CEO and founder of SmarterDiagnostics,[91] a possible starting point is to use the first people involved in testing and feedback, like clinics or labs involved initially, as they had the time to get to know you and therefore might trust you. Moreover, you would have improved the product or service according to their feedback, so it is now probably something they might want. Substantially, they used the first feedback and test users as starting customers.

If we go out of the constrained world of medtech and biotech and we consider companies in general, many popular companies were startups at the beginning, and literally began by gaining their first customers from their circle of friends, colleagues, and schoolmates. It seems this was the case for Facebook and others.[92] Be careful: friends and people who know you might not be a good representative niche preparing you to scale up. Sometimes your friends might be too geeky or have too much of an engineering background, or the other way around, being biased by personal prejudices toward you—both positive or negative.

Next, reaching out to specific unknown people directly via email, social media, direct messaging, and phone calls, is often used. It sounds a bit invasive, and actually it is. There is a thin line, but many high-profile companies did this at the beginning. YouTube is claimed to have individually hunted many Myspace users, and Airbnb went after authors of posts about renting on Craigslist.[93] Substantially, without being invasive, it is a good idea to approach people using a service similar to the one you want to provide and let them know that it exists. This piggybacking or counter-positioning is the expansion of a network using a user's complaint on a known network.

A lighter approach for direct messaging is given by posting kindly on online platforms. Again, there is a thin line between promoting, asking opinions, and spamming. In practice, you should mention your product or idea in specific platforms where potential users hang out, eg Reddit, Product Hunt, Hacker News, university forums, and events, as Dropbox founder Drew Houston is reported to have done.[94]

Lastly, you can use so-called "guerrilla marketing." In guerrilla marketing, the focus is on creating memorable and engaging experiences that generate buzz and word-of-mouth promotion. It often involves using non-traditional marketing channels, such as intensively distributed posters and flyers, street art, or even flash mobs. Guerrilla marketing campaigns are typically designed to be cost-effective, as they rely on creativity and ingenuity rather than large advertising budgets. By leveraging unconventional tactics, social media, and online platforms, guerrilla marketing can reach a wide audience without heavy financial investment. The approach is therefore ideal for products and services that require customers to be related to the local environment. It is nevertheless effective, as it allows them to literally own a physical space.

Apart from guerrilla marketing, old-school pitching can also pay some rewards by targeting specific conferences. Founder of Canva, Melanie Perkins, found that going to local meetups and technical conferences gave her opportunities to meet designers and advertise her platform.[95]

This was not meant to be an exhaustive list. It is just to drive your attention that famous startups, even those that are strictly hi-tech, did not get their customers by just sitting on a chair. Actions need to be taken, otherwise nothing will happen.

Launching the startup

I have recently become interested in clay. I bought five kilograms, I learned the basics of modeling, and which oven to use. I wanted to do something cool, so I went above and beyond. I bought a kintsugi kit (the ancient Japanese art of gluing a broken object with gold – a sort of traumatic growth through objects). My idea was to show a fractured brain looking stronger after a recovery. I broke my piece and glued it with the kintsugi kit. People told me, "It looks disgusting, like someone vomited during an autopsy," but the entire preparation took many weeks: buying clay, learning to model, learning kintsugi, breaking the clay, using kintsugi, finding an oven, using the oven, and so on. Would I have spent all this time if I showed the initial step and got bad feedback? Maybe yes, maybe no.

In the startup universe, life is similar. People spend months or years preparing and refining business models with market analysis based on rough assumptions, with user experience tested only at launch, patents, or other regulations, just to then be disappointed or to pivot and restart.

In practice, there are rules—especially in fintech, biotech, and with drugs development—where there are clinical trials to be performed and regulations to be respected. In those cases, time is needed, but it is also true that it is better to get feedback as early on as possible, even on the first day.

We should not spend time or money building something that nobody wants, or that you have to modify painfully, which will take you a lot of work at that point. With a "lean mentality" you should build a minimum viable product (MVP) (or even less than an MVP), set up a website, avoid unnecessary expenses, and find customers immediately. It is probably better to go beyond this, even creating just a mock-up to show around, so you can see if people are interested or if your idea is not working. If people are interested, they can even subscribe to a waiting list or fund you. If you are providing something useful, people will be willing to pay and give you money upfront. If this does not happen, it is already a mild red flag—maybe nobody will want your product or service once it is up and running in the months or years ahead. Indeed, an MVP is an essential version of a product with minimal usable features to be tested by early users who can then provide feedback.

Consider having different levels of launch, like a pre-launch with initial adapters (or even funders) and then a large-scale launch. Each case is different, and things can be more complicated if related to medtech or fintech regulation, but the idea is still valid: one can launch an alpha/beta/pre-MVP immediately to gauge reactions, and in the meantime proceed with clinical trials, regulations, patents, etc.

In the case of an app related to products and services in this context, there are plenty of services even with no-code, where you can create an app in ten minutes with few programming skills, which you just need to show to your customers (the entire cycle can happen in one day). These are obviously quick solutions; if you need some computer vision, machine learning, or other AI tools, having a software engineer involved is crucial for understanding and managing potential issues that may arise in more complex stages. Even though non-programmers can use these solutions, having a skilled engineer involved early on is recommended to prevent difficulties during advanced stages.

In summary, whatever the business idea is, it is better to launch immediately, at least within a restricted group of users. App prototyping and deploying with no-code or low-code services can literally take one day. Feedback is a relevant aspect of this initial step, and not being blinded by what has been built is critical. It is also important that feedback is collected in a non-biased way, eg an external person or company collects the feedback and then reports back to you. It can be easy to lose perspective when we pour so much energy into building something.

Summary

In this chapter we reviewed practical advice for activists and entrepreneurs on launching a new venture or movement. We emphasized the importance of having a core team of aligned cofounders, defining a "moat" to protect against competition, developing a GTM strategy to acquire initial customers, and launching as early as possible to get feedback and iterate. The advice is to be flexible and pivot based on feedback, rather than getting too attached to initial ideas. These are overall strategic tips for getting a new initiative off the ground and finding product-market fit.

In the next chapter, we will discuss more low-resource settings aspects and we will continue on to more general elements, such as choosing the proper business model.

FIVE

Managing Low-Resource Settings

This is the hardcore part. Some of the content in this chapter will sound odd if you've only lived in high-income countries, while it will resonate if you are from or work in the southern hemisphere. I am not talking about chickens running in the street or goats roaming around. There are customs and rules in rural areas we have to follow, and other aspects like pricing we need to take into account.

Approaching rural communities

You might think that registering a company, obtaining an ethical approval, or getting medtech certification is a nightmare. If you live in the southern hemisphere and you want to operate in rural areas, there are additional layers. Rural areas might still follow ancient local communities' rules, with chiefs, traditions, and venerable ways of doing things. You cannot simply go to the clinic operating in the area and do your clinical trial or sell goods without following the local rules. Sometimes even just putting a billboard with your company's name on trees can require the local chiefs' authorization.

Like it or not, local stakeholders are the main authority – in some cases even overtaking official authorities. If you want to operate your business or social change, or conduct your clinical trial, you literally need to go and speak with the chief of the community first. At least, this was my experience in sub-Saharan Africa until 2018. Once the local stakeholder's approval is granted, you can then proceed.

Sometimes, the chiefs will like the idea of having something new in their community so much, they will organize a community assembly to introduce yourself and the thing you are launching, as shown in the photograph above. This varies on a case-by-case basis, which companies operating in those areas know well. It also creates a level of cooperation, rather than representing you arriving as a white man, imposing your business and exploiting them. You need to be introduced in some way in the local rural areas, otherwise despite all your official approval, things will be stopped or you will face issues. Instead of giving an example from somebody else, in the following section I report probably the most interesting project I conducted.

A special case has been all interactions with Chinese companies arriving in sub-Saharan Africa with affordable prices for services and products[96] (this is a story on its own beyond the purpose of this chapter). I do not have direct experiences, but similar circumstances apply also for Latin America and South Asia.

In summary, if you are planning to run a business or project in those areas, you need to consider this additional step in your budget and timeline. Failing to follow local customs might delay or even stop your project or business. Please understand that I am not referring to any kind of bribery, I am referring to cooperating with local stakeholders according to the traditions.

The DocmeUp experience

There is currently a severe shortage of medical staff, and child mortality is still quite high. For instance, in Ghana only 54% of women attend the minimum number of four prenatal visits.[97] In rural areas, the distance to modern antenatal care providers can be considerable. Pregnant women might have to travel more than 15 kilometers to a modern healthcare provider.

Dr Crimi during an assembly in a rural community to discuss the DocmeUp Project

In 2013 I received some funding from the Technical School of Switzerland to conduct a cooperation project in Ghana – more specifically a prenatal-care project using biomedical tools. The goal was to increase antenatal care for women in rural areas, and to provide affordable telemedicine. Activities spanned between 2014 and 2016.

The project comprised training women (called community health workers) living in the local communities so that they could keep track of pregnant women in their community through a mobile phone app, and, when necessary, remind them to go to their prenatal visits. In cases where women were not in a condition to do so, ultrasound scans would be acquired in the rural community. In practice, the app given to the community health workers also created a calendar for trained technicians who could visit rural areas with portable ultrasound machines, sending scans to gynecologists in urban areas who could alert them to take further action when danger to the mother or fetus was detected. In its pilot version, the project was covered by a research grant, while potential scaling was aimed at being entrusted to the government and sponsors.

I had an ethical approval by the local institutional review board (Noguchi Memorial Institute for Medical Research in Accra) to run this project. However, it was my first in-field project and I had no idea how to practically run it. I attended a course on rural health, where the process of asking permission of local stakeholders respected by the rural community was explained. Despite the fact that I was in possession of all official paperwork, I had to be introduced to the local chief of each community where the pilot was taking place, to explain the rationale and steps of the process and get their approval. Luckily, thanks to networking, I was introduced smoothly to the local chiefs and the project proceeded with only minor delays.

This was an enriching experience. At that time I was assisted by some of my students who volunteered to come and talk to each village chief with me (you have to understand that in Ghanaian I am an "Obruni," a white man), while some former students were hired as research assistants to report the study from an epidemiological point of view. Generally, chiefs were interested in listening to my ideas and the project, and after the traditional interactions, they honorably granted me access to their communities. I was even sometimes invited afterwards to introduce myself during a town assembly to explain the project. In other cases, there were town criers or local radio that would spread the noise that something new was happening in the area. All this was "very colorful" and charming.

An anecdotal aspect worth sharing is that the chiefs are generally educated people who can speak English well, though the interactions normally take place in the local language (Twi in my case), and an interpreter is required, even if the chief speaks English. In some cases, the interpreter might act as an adviser, discussing with the chief if there are any issues that seem dodgy. This is the custom.

The last mile supply chain issue

Imagine a device or a vaccine has been designed in Switzerland, produced in Taiwan, and moved to a storage facility in Germany near an airport. Now it is finally time for it to be sent to Coco, a community doctor in Pumayacu (a little village not far from Iquitos in Peru). Pumayacu has no land connection; for something to arrive, it has to travel by plane to Iquitos and then on small boats entering the capillary branches of the Amazon River.

Now imagine the vaccine has to reach Kafui, a Ghanian community health practitioner. The goods have to land in Accra (the capital of Ghana) and a truck has to travel through bumpy roads, unpaved yet jammed with cars, to reach Nyadieya, a little village on the way toward Kumasi.

Do you see where the bottleneck is? It is not between Taiwan and Germany, and it is not between Germany and Iquitos or Accra. The last mile issue refers to the final stage of a distribution process, where products or services are delivered to end users or customers. In low-income countries, the last mile poses a significant challenge within the supply chain, like the steps between Iquitos and Pumayacu or Accra and Nyadieya. In low-income countries, this last stage is more cumbersome than all previous steps and often encounters various obstacles, including inadequate infrastructure, limited connectivity, and logistical challenges. It seems those are unrelated issues to entrepreneurs creating innovation, but if your end users are located in places like Pumayacu or Nyadieya, the last mile issue has to be considered in designing a product, and considered in your business plan.

The causes of the last mile issue are generally related to inadequate infrastructure: insufficient road networks, poor transportation systems, and lack of storage facilities hindering efficient delivery and distribution of goods. Surprisingly, this final step in the supply chain is the most complicated. Low-income countries have advanced notably in mobile connectivity, though some areas are still underserved. Inaccessible or unreliable communication networks make it difficult to track shipments, coordinate deliveries, and handle customer inquiries effectively.

The last mile issue hampers business growth and market penetration. It limits the ability of companies to reach customers in remote areas, reducing their market potential and revenue. Sadly, this is not just a business matter, it also impacts social development: inadequate access to essential products, such as healthcare supplies and educational resources, can negatively impact the quality of life for individuals in low-income countries. Lastly, environmental concerns are present, since inefficient last-mile delivery contributes to increased carbon emissions and environmental degradation, exacerbating climate change.

The "cold" supply chain is even worse. When we use the term "cold chain," we refer to a temperature-controlled supply chain that is specifically designed to maintain the integrity and quality of perishable goods, certain foods (not just ice-cream), medicines, and other temperature-sensitive items, from the production starting point to the end user. To prevent spoilage, deterioration, or loss of potency, it is essential that this unique supply chain instance includes a number of operations for storage, transit, and distribution where temperature is meticulously managed and tracked.

To maintain a product's safety, effectiveness, and quality, it is important to keep it within a certain temperature range—otherwise, what would be the point of delivering an expensive novel vaccine or enzyme when the active ingredient is not useful anymore? In practice, this frequently entails the employment of specialized tools like cold storage facilities, refrigerated transportation, and temperature-monitoring tools. Since even slight fluctuations from the advised temperature range can have a major impact on a product's quality and effectiveness, keeping a cold chain is essential for products that are sensitive to temperature changes. Imagine you want to distribute a vaccine and / or some specific reagents for diagnostics in rural areas in places with high temperatures (eg sub-Saharan Africa, Latin America, or Bali). Not only might the roads be bumpy and cumbersome but you would also need to have specific fridge cells running continuously. As you can imagine, this adds considerable costs. Indeed, many pharmaceutical companies forgo operating in these rural areas as it is not financially rewarding, given the additional costs. They cannot simply increase the prices as there will be no demand at a reasonable price for them.

This is the moment where you need to think like Mac-Gyver. You have to come up with solutions that fit all those constraints. In the case of vaccines or chemical reagents, solutions can be given by the lyophilization of the reagents.[98] Lyophilization, also known as freeze drying, is the process of removing water from the reagents or medicines, which allows them to be stored at more affordable temperatures for longer. This be achieved by specific devices – some of which are affordable on the market. Alternative ideas can also be given by novel technologies, such as drones that can fly at certain altitudes with lower temperatures, or avoiding traffic jams or bad road conditions. This has been the rationale behind Zipline, a company operating in Rwanda and other countries in collaboration with the global alliance for vaccination. They experimented with the delivery of many drugs, and even COVID-19 samples.[99] As with many other things, in every challenge lies an opportunity.

The bottom of the pyramid

Coimbatore Krishnarao Prahalad was an Indian-American economist and expert of corporate strategy. He was born in what is now Tamil Nadu, India, and he was a professor at the Stephen Ross School of Business at the University of Michigan, US. He was another prominent figure of the eradicating poverty through business world, introducing the concept of the bottom to the pyramid economy:[100]

If we look at the actual distribution of wealth in the world, we can see that a few of the richest people of the planet are on top (Elon Musk, Jeff Bezos, Larry Page, Warren Buffet, etc). Next we have a slightly larger group of people representing the 10% of the population (627 million people) handling 40% of the entire wealth of the planet, followed by a third level including the 33% of the population that hold 13% of the world's wealth. Lastly, at the bottom, 2.8 billion people live with the remaining 1%. Practically, the majority of people on the planet is made up of people living with less than USD$2 per day, as is idealistically depicted in the figure below.

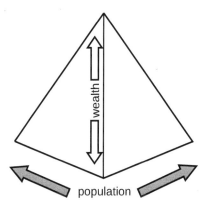

Idealization of the pyramid of wealth

Professor Prahalad proposed that businesses, governments, and donor agencies stop thinking of the poor as victims and instead start seeing them as resilient, creative entrepreneurs and value-demanding consumers. After all, they are the largest population of the planet and it would be a pity to neglect this huge potential market. Indeed, this thinking brought a series of innovations such as microcredit and market-specific products.

Microcredit is one example of "bottom of the pyramid." It was introduced in South Asia and then spread to Africa and South America, and it captured worldwide attention when Muhammad Yunus won the Nobel Peace Prize for creating economic and social development from the bottom. Microcredit means providing small loans or other financial services to low-income individuals or groups who lack access to traditional banking services. Those people can receive small loans offering little guarantees (eg a cheap motor scooter).[101]

Market-specific products are products designed with the needs and financial availability of the poor in mind. For example, an affordable shampoo that works best with cold water and is sold in small packets to reduce barriers of upfront costs for the poor.[102]

Doing business for the "bottom of the pyramid" is difficult, not only in terms of regulations and legal constraints but also because the "customers" are not the same as in high-income countries. The difference in income is the least of their differences. They can have different cultures, ways of perceiving quantity, or even prejudices on novel solutions. For instance, if a European or American want to sell something to be used in a household in India, it can be in a completely different context: the stove might have a different organization, the floor might be dissimilar, or access to electricity might be reduced. There are so many things that we cannot easily anticipate and these do not stop at the low accessible price. It is not enough to understand the household or the ideal customer. Local context, such as the community or neighborhood, has to be taken into account. Their day-to-day activities are different than in Europe. If just giving financial incentives (as mentioned in Chapter 1) was hard, designing products to be bought voluntarily by people in low-income areas is even more demanding.

Nevertheless, as Prahalad pointed out, we have a huge market at the bottom of the pyramid and it will be a pity to simply ignore it.

Embrace Global

Embrace Global was founded in 2008 by Jane Chen, Linus Liang, Naganand Murty, and Rahul Panicker.[103] The company is headquartered in Boston, Massachusetts. Embrace develops innovative products to address health challenges in developing countries. The company's main product is a portable infant warmer, designed to prevent hypothermia in premature and low-birth-weight babies. It has been used in low-income counties, such as in sub-Saharan Africa, and in war-affected areas where clinics often had electricity shortages, such as in Ukraine during the Russian military aggression.

The innovation

- The Embrace infant warmer is a low-cost portable device that helps to regulate a newborn's temperature. More specifically, it is a sleeping-bag-like pouch with a thermostat and a phase change material (ie a special wax) that can maintain a constant temperature for several hours. It is designed to run even with unstable electricity.
- The warmer does not require electricity and is safe, reusable, and portable. It is designed to be used in remote clinics with unstable power infrastructure.

Challenges faced

- Lack of ideal distribution model to reach the last mile, especially considering distribution within war zones.
- Creating awareness about the affordable warmer.
- Scaling up its business due to the costs involved.

Business model and success factors

- The company clearly focuses mostly on the bottom of the pyramid, though not strictly on business to customer.
- The infant warmer costs around USD$200, which is less than 1% of the cost of a traditional incubator. Embrace partners with local hospitals and distributors to get the product to end users.

Impact

- Since launching, it is estimated that Embrace has helped over 200,000 babies until 2023. Clinical trials found Embrace to have 100% efficacy in regulating body temperature.

- Embrace has received funding from organizations like USAID and Bill & Melinda Gates Foundation, and individuals like Jeff Bezos. It indirectly involves the bottom of the pyramid.

Key takeaways

- Embrace successfully developed an innovative low-cost medical device to address newborn hypothermia for low-resource settings.

- The company is based on a social entrepreneurship model to make the product accessible and sustainable, though it considers clinics and hospitals as the customers, not individuals living in low-resource areas. Indeed, it cannot be considered as directly targeting the bottom of the pyramid; it can be seen as an indirect impact on the bottom of the pyramid.

- Nevertheless, Embrace's infant warmer has had significant social impact. It demonstrated that uncomplicated, affordable innovations can help solve major global health challenges, not only in the low-income countries but also in other contexts in cases of need.

Summary

In this chapter we discussed strategies for doing business and implementing projects in rural, low-income regions, which have additional challenges compared to urban areas. We emphasized the importance of cooperating with local stakeholders such as village chiefs to gain approval before starting operations. Other key issues included the "last mile" supply chain difficulties in getting products to remote areas, the large market potential of the "bottom of the pyramid" low-income populations, and the need to design affordable and culturally appropriate products and services for people with limited incomes.

I hope that after reading this you are more aware of the obstacles but also the opportunities in bringing innovation to low-resourced rural communities.

SIX

Nailing The Nuts And Bolts

This chapter is focused on specific details related to strategical choices. These are probably not the most intriguing aspects of a venture, but nevertheless they are critical aspects to be carefully taken into consideration. Indeed, in a venture, we need to choose the used business model—what will be our exist or growth strategy—and establish whether we will need certifications.

Business models

What is a business model? A business model describes in detail how a corporation develops, distributes, and acquires value in the market. It acts as a manual for how a company runs, makes money, and maintains profitability. A well-defined business model outlines the key aspects of a company's operations, including its target customer segments, value proposition, revenue sources, cost structure, and distribution channels. It is, in practice, the way the company makes money – substantially, how interactions between customers, the company, and other external stakeholders happen.[104]

If we were selling pineapples along the roads in Kigali or Delhi, the business model is a clear sales-driven model; you have costs to grow the pineapples, and the difference between your sales and your costs defines your income. In our evolved and convoluted world, things are more complicated. Companies operating in different fields might have different business models, but in the same field there can also be differences. For instance, Microsoft and Facebook plainly have different business models: one uses advertisements; the other sells goods. Another fundamental difference is whether a company aims at other businesses—business to business (B2B)—or individuals—business to customer (B2C). The number of business models that have been used in different contexts probably ranges between seventy and eighty. Indeed, new business models are created by novel technologies, societal shifts, and even merely new online platforms.

In this chapter we cannot explore all possible models, from franchising to community models. Also, because cultures are dynamic, consequently new business models can pop every day. I just mention the interesting ones at the moment. Even this list might become outdated in a few years; some are specific to physical stores and some are exclusively online. The options in medtech and biotech are somewhat more limited to product providers (direct selling), licensees, and acquisition models, while in more general context there are further possibilities. Nevertheless, the focus should remain on whether the product being offered satisfies a genuine market need before making your decision.

The product providers model

The product providers (or direct selling, or retailer) model is the most traditional. It includes the initial example of selling pineapples. Depending on the type of goods, there are different undertones, for instance, disposable and reusable products. Disposable products (like syringes) require generally high sales volumes due to the low margin or return associated, and they have to be easy to use. Reusable products are generally more expensive and often require associated training, such as an ultrasound machine or MRI scan.

The brokerage model

This business model, known by the name "brokerage business model," takes inspiration from the finance world. It is used by service companies that act as an intermediary between buyers and sellers of different assets, including stocks, bonds, real estate, commodities, and more. By connecting buyers and sellers, brokers facilitate transactions while collecting a commission or other charge for their assistance.

More generally, this model can be expanded to contexts other than finance. For instance, a consulting firm may charge a customer to set up and grant access to a third-party cloud provider. This is how your company is focused on bringing together buyers (your customers) and additional sellers to conduct commerce. The actual subject of the brokerage can be both a product or a service.

The license model

The license model is predicated on the notion of producing a good, like a software or picture, and then making numerous copies available for usage by businesses or individuals. The license may be time limited or permanent, or it may be restricted to a certain number of users.

The acquisition model

This is perhaps specific to research and cutting-edge innovation, such as new drugs. The idea behind the acquisition model is that the entire innovative company is the product, given a precious innovation correlated by a patent and highly skilled staff. The whole startup reaches maturity, and then can be "sold" to larger corporation in the exit strategy.

The community business model

Also known as the (online) community-driven business model, the community business model is centered on forging and maintaining an active community of people with comparable goals, ideologies, or interests. This strategy emphasizes getting people involved in the community and making them feel like they belong, which promotes various forms of collaboration, support, and moneymaking for the business. Examples include Etsy, Redbubble, and even Airbnb.

This model focuses on encouraging people to feel a sense of community and connection when they are brought together by similar interests, objectives, or values. By using the power of social networks and word of mouth, businesses can build a strong community around a product or service, using this to grow their clientele and revenue.

The community model strongly emphasizes the value of incorporating user feedback and input into the creation and improvement of goods and services, in addition to promoting a sense of community. By actively seeking out and incorporating user recommendations, businesses may demonstrate their commitment to addressing the interests and preferences of their community members. This strategy not only produces a more positive and individualized user experience, but it also promotes the feelings of pride and loyalty among community members because they can see that their opinions are being acknowledged and taken into account.

In conclusion, the community model is a company model that relies on loyal customers and strong social ties to provide income. This model can span widely, including products or services. Businesses can inspire long-term adherence to their goods or services by doing three things:

1. Fostering a sense of community

2. Creating an engaging and encouraging environment

3. Aggressively soliciting consumer feedback

The advertising model

Some businesses utilize the advertising model as a means of generating income to market brands, products, and services on their own spaces. Businesses use this method to offer advertising time or space to other companies. This paradigm is followed by some TV programs and websites, all social media platforms (such as Facebook, Instagram, and YouTube), some SaaS companies providing services, and a large number of news websites. However, email marketing is becoming more popular. They frequently charge their clients based on cost per click, cost per action, and cost per impression.

The franchise model

This is typical of restaurants and certain clothes chains. With franchising, we sell a successful approach and branding to someone else; in practice, we grant access to a successful model already tested and known. This is generally deployed into the real world with physical premises, rather than online. The franchise model can in turn repeat a product or service provider model. It can be a chain of stores or restaurants, or a chain of services, such as real estate agents.

The merchant model

This model is represented by the case of a company that provides services and sells goods where the merchant is responsible for the products. Amazon and Walmart fall into this category, while eBay is an extreme case as it allows even private individuals to sell their goods and hold auctions.

As an alternative, some companies employ the so-called linked business model, which is predicated on the notion of compensating or rewarding affiliates who can refer customers to them. Dealing with this mindset will provide you with an endless array of possibilities for buying.

Affiliate marketing works similarly to sponsored partnerships in that it enlists outside parties to market your company on your behalf. You can work with affiliates to market your items on blogs, social media, and other online channels by putting affiliate marketing into practice. The promoter can be compensated for their contributions using affiliate links, which are special URLs that track purchases. The method for calculating revenues may resemble the advertising model. This strategy is used by both established e-commerce sites like Amazon and emerging platforms looking to expand. For instance, they give you a proportion of the profits if you refer new paying subscribers or if a product is sold as a result of a link you posted on your blog.

The subscription model

Last but not the least, the subscription model is a business model in which customers pay a recurring fee at regular intervals (such as monthly or annually) to access a product or service. Newspapers and magazines, as well as Netflix, Amazon Prime, and Spotify, are examples of companies that use this approach.

Even medtech companies, which sell a device followed by complementary supports or necessary add-ons that are consumed, rapidly fall into this category as well. For example, a company might sell a diagnostic device as a traditional purchase business model, then necessary cartridges for this device are given and paid for monthly. In doing this, the subscription model in turn includes a perpetual direct selling model of reusable goods or services.

Any subscription-based strategy that seeks to keep users engaged and satisfied over time must prioritize customer retention. By focusing on delivering exceptional customer experience, resolving difficulties, and consistently improving the product, businesses may convince customers to keep using the service. Retaining consumers helps the business expand and become more profitable by decreasing churn rates and increasing lifetime value of each subscriber.

Subscription-based businesses need to implement effective client onboarding and retention procedures if they want consumers to remain interested in and committed to the platform. This tactic increases subscriber lifetime value while also increasing customer satisfaction, which promotes long-term corporate success.

Taking into account these models before starting your organization can significantly influence your style and impact your choices. Yet models are not strict; individuals can adjust to their unique circumstances and even design hybrid situations that generate income.

Survival and exit strategies

Finding a need or a gap in the market and having a related successful solution is a good start. A successful business model, initial investments, and a first customer is also promising, although this is just the beginning—there is yet a distance to travel before a firm becomes successful. There is a fundamental strategical aspect that we need to consider now: in which direction do you want to go? Do you want to one day be bought out or will you continue to expand and eventually make an initial public offering (IPO)? An IPO is the process through which a private company becomes publicly traded on a stock exchange. Aiming for an IPO might be the most alluring option because you largely maintain control of the business and can probably continue to expand, but the reality is that a startup can collapse at any point.

I once made an investment in Uniti AB, a small, reasonably priced electric car firm, through an angels-crowdfunding site. The Uniti One was marketed as a stylishly constructed tiny electric vehicle with three seats and a 50 kW small battery that should enable travel between 150 and 300 kilometers. The retail price was planned around EUR€17,000. Uniti AB had three rounds of funding through channels for angel investors and crowdsourcing: one unidentified, one of around UK £1 million, and one of 2.5 million Swedish Kronor. However, more liquidity was required. They ultimately failed and eventually filed for bankruptcy.[105] This scenario should alert you that bankruptcy may occur at any point, even after a respectable round of investment.

Sometimes choosing to be acquired is a wise decision. However, loss of control occurs when you are acquired. Your business is no longer yours; you merely represent a smaller portion. As a founder, you should be aware of the advantages and constraints between being acquired and reaching an IPO. Let's talk about the two approaches' respective strategies.

Once you have reached a certain level of maturity (usually further research or more patents, certification, or permission), you can build on the initial investments with other rounds of funding or income to be bought. Acquisition is relevant for large companies, as once a company grows a lot in size they tend to have difficulty in generating novel intellectual property from the inside, while acquisition provides a fast track to achieving this for them. In fact, businesses frequently buy startups to obtain access to cutting-edge technologies, boost their market share, or diversify their portfolio of goods and services.

Popular examples are GitHub, YouTube, and Instagram:

- Facebook spent more than USD $1 billion to buy the popular photo-sharing service Instagram in 2012.[106]

- Google purchased the video-sharing website YouTube for USD $1.65 billion in 2006.[107] Thanks to this acquisition, Google was able to strengthen its position in online video and increase the number of advertising possibilities available.

- Microsoft bought the GitHub software development platform in 2018 for USD $7.5 billion.[108]

In those and other cases, the acquired companies were already known and successful and probably approached by the larger company.

If this is not your case, to get acquired, the steps are the same as a usual pitch (demonstrate value proposition, personalize outreach, etc). The key decision-makers should be identified in place of investors; research and locate the key decision-makers within the target companies once you have identified them. These decision-makers could include executives, CEOs, heads of departments, or relevant contacts who have the authority to make acquisition decisions. LinkedIn, company websites, and industry networks can be valuable resources for finding the right individuals.

Independently, whether the goal is acquisition or ultimately an IPO, the first phase of the startup funding cycle is pre-seed funding. Pre-seed funding is commonly given to startups before they even have a concept or an MVP. Pre-seed capital is typically provided by the company's founders, their families, and the occasional angel investor who wants to invest early. Alternatively, the founding team seeks funding from investors already at the pre-seed stage (this is indeed a growing behavior currently) to raise the funds necessary to set up the company's fundamental infrastructure. It is also widely used to develop the MVP and accomplish early objectives like acquiring the first client and investing money on marketing. Typically, a pre-seed funding campaign will raise anything between USD $150K and $1 million (but often much less than this range). However, the number of investors participating in the pre-seed investment stage is increasing.

People are increasingly validating the viability of businesses without investing time in creating prototypes or obtaining certification, which may be pointless, using pre-seed market analysis without MVP. The typical starting point for investors is seed cash. In general, angel investors dominated this stage, but venture capitalists started to recognize the value of accepting risk by assisting businesses in their early phases of viability. However, only angel investors will take the firm seriously if it lacks strong intellectual property, clinical trials, and a measurable moat. At this stage, founders will be seeking to fund between USD$1 million and $5 million. Numbers in Europe can be meager compared to the US approach, therefore double registration of the company in the US might be worth consideration.

At this stage of funding, the startup has between two and ten employees; it will onboard its first clients after refining the MVP to be more market-fit. A company obtaining Series A funding has a finished product, a clientele, and a clear expansion strategy. In general, it should appear more like a flourishing company than a scruffy startup. Even if revenues are small, they should be consistent; the business should have a long-term growth strategy in place (rather than a GTM strategy), and it should preserve liquidity until income is enough to support the operation on its own.

Seed capital is easier to obtain than Series A funding. Fewer than half of all startups with seed capital get Series A funding. Given that Series A funding is far more considerable (USD$15 million to $20 million), investors will require more evidence to convince them of the startup's potential. Most startups do not manage to proceed further, or now consider the safer opportunity of acquisition. Few lucky ones are able to get into IPO after Series A, though there are exceptions. Most companies will not have the size or consistency needed to qualify for listing right after Series A.

By the time a company is looking for Series B funding, it has already proven itself. The prospect for additional expansion is obvious, the client base is expanding, and the product-market fit has been confirmed. Although Series B fundraising can range from USD$15 million to $900 million, it's paradoxical that founders typically find this round of funding to be much simpler than Series A. There are also fewer venture capitalists able to handle this level of capital. Investors recognize that a startup that has advanced to this degree is a relatively safe venture, and at this time you are gaining the attention of the large institutional players.

Generally, Series C is the last investment cycle, though many organizations also pursue Series D, E, and F rounds. The largest investment round, Series C, can range in size from USD$30 million to multiple billions of dollars. The Series C money will be used by the founders to grow even more internationally, enter new industries, buy smaller companies, and create new products and services for the market. The business is now an established and successful enterprise rather than still being a startup. As for the previous stage, there are fewer and fewer venture capitalists with the capacity of investing in a Series C.

The process of going public and becoming a publicly traded corporation is the last step for the majority of enterprises. The company will use the substantial new funds it receives from the IPO in a way that is comparable to how it would use Series C capital. It will be used to support expansion through the introduction of new products, markets, and acquisitions of other younger startups (yes, we are entering the loop now).

Since they will make big profits from the business they worked so hard to create from the ground up, many entrepreneurs decide to sell their businesses at the IPO. Some will carry on serving in leadership or advisory roles. Startup founders are usually aware of the advantages of handing the reins of a publicly traded company to a seasoned CEO, though. If it helps, an IPO typically involves the following steps: choosing a bank, pricing, stabilization, transition, due diligence, and filings. If the market capitalization of an IPO is equal to or greater than the market capitalization of the competitors in the industry, it is deemed successful. Market capitalization can be estimated as the product between the stock price and total number of company's outstanding shares.

A modern company will go through four or five rounds of investment before they are prepared to go public, depending on whether they seek pre-seed funding right away or not. Sometimes a startup will take part in a Series D, E, or F round of investment, or it may be prepared earlier. All of these steps take time, so setbacks are to be expected, particularly at the beginning.

Certification

Paradromics[109] is a company producing innovative brain implants, which have managed to get closer to an FDA approval. While the need for certification for an invasive device that touches the brain is obvious, many people are unaware that certification is also necessary for other seemingly innocent gadgets, such as thermometers. Nowadays, even AI-based diagnostic tools require certification to be taken seriously.

Often we see popularized new diagnostic solutions in the news, in research papers, and on social media. However, those are not always immediately applicable in clinics. Before an innovation can be trusted by medical experts worldwide, it must be certified because some of them may be used to analyze vital signals or perform life-threatening functions, such as a pacemaker. Indeed, there are classifications of risk. Medical devices can typically be divided into three categories based on the degree of danger associated with them, ranging from low-risk apparatus like medical thermometers, disposable gloves, or tongue depressors to high-risk implants like pacemakers that are necessary to preserve life.

Occasionally, uncertified equipment is used with an explicit warning and consent of the non-certification is acquired. This may be a temporary solution for a startup business with limited resources. They introduce "a research product" that is nonetheless put to use, and in the interim, they begin the correct certification process. The number of investors, clinical partners, and clients can all be significantly reduced by a lack of accreditation, but it can still be a start. Considering we are talking about health, it is strongly recommended to give a disclaimer about the lack of certification.

Certifications slightly vary whether they are issued in the US, Europe, or somewhere else. The FDA is in charge of making sure that new medical innovations made available to patients in the US are secure and efficient. The FDA has jurisdiction over a wide range of goods that collectively account for a quarter of all consumer expenditure in the US. It oversees the production, testing, and sales of chemical and biological agents as well as medical equipment. The Conformité Européenne (CE) mark, which is comparable in the European economic area to the FDA mark in the US, must be visible on any medical equipment marketed in the European Union. If one of those certificates already exists, certain African and Asian nations will give a local certificate almost straightforwardly. The UK might be a more complicated case at the time of writing, as they need to revalidate the CE mark according to their legislation, which is more complex than those of average African countries.

A more complex nightmare is presented if the innovation is conceived totally from a low-income country outside of the US and Europe. Whereas medical devices have considerable challenges in Europe or the US to get certified, at least there is a path. For medical innovation completely created in sub-Saharan countries, even the pathways are not clear. Uganda is generally not considered the wealthiest country in Africa. However, Makerere University in Kampala, Uganda, can boast several outstanding scientists that have even produced considerable innovations, some of which were attempted to be translated into medical devices used by physicians. Some researchers of the College of Health Sciences at Makerere University have conducted a survey with the aim of clarifying the perspective of getting certified in Uganda, rather than obtaining an FDA or CE certification and then coming back to be approved in Uganda.[110] After all, FDA and CE are certifications for the US and Europe; why shouldn't Africa have its own system? The survey highlighted that there is a lack of clear know-how. Even the local national drug policy and authority reported no clear provision to authorize medical devices. Support for innovators should be provided to collaborate with social scientists for the proper translation into the real world—there is still room for improvement.

For the CE certification, the European Commission Regulation No. 2017/745 has to be followed for medical devices,[111] the No. 2017/746 for in-vitro diagnostic devices,[112] and Directive 2001/83/EC for medicinal products that include a medical device (combination products eg medicine and device).[113]

Devices can be classified according to classes: Class I (sterile, measuring, or reusable surgical instruments), Class IIa, Class IIb, or Class III. Links to those regulations are given in the Further Reading section. For the FDA, a similar classification exists, except for the distinction IIa and IIb, which exists only in Europe and Canada. Businesses often employ the EN ISO 13485 standard to achieve compliance. In most cases, you need a quality management system (QMS) in place to obtain FDA approval for a medical device, as the FDA requires medical device manufacturers to adhere to specific quality system regulations.

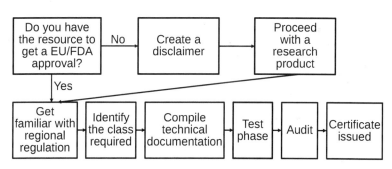

Simplistic view of the certification process

It is crucial to remember that depending on the nation or region you are in, the particular criteria and procedures may change. I provide here a general description of the procedures needed to receive such a certificate, also depicted in the figure above.

1. Become familiar with the rules and specifications that apply to the specific country or state where you aim to sell the designed product. These rules might cover biomedical device-specific safety requirements, documentation requirements, testing protocols, and quality control measures.

2. Understand which certification class is needed. In practice, according to the risk posed by the device, this is which class the device to be certified belongs to.

3. Compile the technical documentation, which heavily depends on the deemed class. This normally consists of test results, design specifications, manufacturing procedures, risk analyses, and clinical evaluations.

4. A testing phase for the biomedical device can start. This could entail doing laboratory testing, performance analyses, and safety evaluations. You could be required to use an authorized testing laboratory for certain tests.

5. While doing this, to guarantee the consistency and quality of your biomedical equipment, you need to establish a strong QMS, as a certification

body or registrar will audit the performance of your organization against the latest version of the standards.

6. If your application is approved and your device meets the necessary requirements, you will be issued a biomedical certificate, which might contain specific restrictions or conditions imposed by the regulatory authority.

Building trust

This is not exactly an element of strategy, but more a mindset to be used to grow. For any business, having a powerful brand is essential. Branding means having a marketing strategy that makes a company's identity memorable. This identity includes the company's overall personality as well as its logo, colors, and vision. The idea is to develop a brand that customers would identify as desirable and of high quality.

Effective branding, above all, leaves a mark. Customers will not remember generic or forgettable brands in a crowded market. Conversely, a well-thought-out brand identity sets a business apart. Features that aid in brand recognition and recall include memorable names, visually appealing logos, and a consistent palette and slogans. The brand benefits from this over generic rivals.

Branding also communicates an organization's values. Customers can discern the brand's values from the colors, language, and tone employed in marketing materials. Young, fun branding, for instance, can point to a business with a laid-back, exuberant vibe. Refined aesthetic and high-end materials suggest an elite sensibility.

As mentioned earlier, the other main purpose of branding is to foster loyalty. Customers might return to a brand if they have had a positive experience with it. Familiar names are more likely to be trusted than generic or unfamiliar ones. By doing this, branding builds corporate equity and discourages customers from looking elsewhere. Higher lifetime value per client results from this.

Finally, careful branding inspires and unites staff members. A coherent focus is established across marketing, operations, customer service, and other areas with a strong brand identity. Employee engagement is boosted by their sense of pride in representing a brand they identify with and better client experiences result from this. By using purposeful, strategic branding, businesses can connect emotionally, communicate their values, stand out from the competition, and stimulate economic success.

Generally speaking, branding is linked to gradually developing trust. When you start a new business you meet a series of challenges. For example, customers must be convinced to utilize your products or services and to spread the word about their idea. It is necessary to establish confidence from the beginning. A GTM strategy is the beginning; you need to keep growing. Here are some essential pointers for a new business looking to establish reputation and reliability.

During and after a GTM strategy, we present us to the world. Hence, the need to focus on transparency in all of your messaging and marketing is critical. You have to clearly communicate details about who founded the company, how you operate, where you are located, and what your core values are. Certifications, or lack of them through warnings, should be stated clearly. Many startups fall into the trap of over-hyping themselves and making bold claims that fail to match reality. Instead, be conservative in the promises you make to avoid disappointing people later, then impress them by actually exceeding expectations. This builds positive word-of-mouth.

Make sure your website design instills confidence by looking polished, professional, and secure. Include details on the encryption standards, safe payment methods, and data privacy safeguards you have in place to protect customer information. These details reassure visitors. Proactively ask for and highlight positive customer reviews and testimonials. This offers vital social proof endorsing your business. Seeing other satisfied customers builds trust in potential buyers. Just make sure the testimonials seem authentic and come from real people. Respond promptly and thoughtfully to any customer questions or concerns.

Having accessible customer service through channels like social media, live chat, email, and phone makes you seem reliable and accountable. Take action to address issues instead of letting them linger. Partnering with trusted companies and organizations when possible is great idea. Affiliations with credible names bring some of their reputation to your startup by association. Even small partnerships help in the early stages.

Summary

In this chapter we discussed some critical details that we have to consider within our strategy: critical startup strategy considerations related to business models, funding, certifications, exit planning, branding, and trust.

The choice of different business models will heavily influence our revenues, hence it required particular attention. We revised the steps involved in startup funding, from pre-seed funding through to IPO. The importance of obtaining proper certifications like FDA approval was highlighted. Moreover, strategies for aiming for acquisition versus IPO were outlined.

The text also provided tips for building a strong brand and establishing trustworthiness as a new company through transparency, delivering on promises, professional presentation, customer reviews, responsive customer service, and partnerships. This should conclude general aspects relevant to both high- and low- income countries.

In the next chapters we can go more specifically into IT and AI solutions, as well as paying attention to sustainability.

PART THREE
FROM AI TO SUSTAINABILITY

W hen we talk about "leapfrogging" we do not refer to animals jumping; the term actually belongs to the economy and development. It refers to the introduction of a new technology or policy by skipping inferior, less efficient, more expensive, or polluting technologies and industries and moving directly to more advanced, cheaper, more efficient, and sustainable ones.

Let's take the example of the phone landline in sub-Saharan Africa. For years, people had bad or non-existing phone landlines, and internet connection in certain rural areas was a dream, then mobile phones and related wireless connectivity came. It was cheaper, more accessible, and literally democratized communication.

In this part of the book we first discuss possible information technology solutions that can be accessible in low-resource settings, leading to more efficient outcomes. Then, we move into analyzing decoupling between sustainability and innovation.

SEVEN
Innovation In
The Digital Age

I n this book, we often mention SaaS as an established
way to create a business or handle innovation. The
acronym SaaS stands for "Software as a Service."
Software applications are made available via the internet on a subscription basis in this cloud computing
approach. Users can access and utilize the software
using a web browser rather than installing and maintaining it on each of their computers or servers. The
software is often hosted and managed by a third-party
provider, relieving users of the burden of hardware
and software maintenance. In our fast-paced society, new and more efficient hardware is developed
constantly, making the possession of hardware like

a constant "tax" related to continuously updating it. Many websites are SaaS and the most common business model is the subscription model. Often, those business have no patent and the moat is given by the network effects of subscribers.

The SaaS model has now become affordable, and it can also be implemented by people living in the Global South or with limited resources. However, many elements that are needed to run an SaaS business are still relatively costly for widespread acceptance in developing economies, despite having established industry standards in developed areas.

Although local SaaS providers may have a cost advantage, cloud services are still prohibitively expensive. Low connectivity and frequent power outages restrict the market that software can reach in Africa and rural Latin America, regardless of whether it is domestically produced or imported. The real cost of using SaaS is significantly greater due to backup power source expenses. Indeed, related infrastructures, such as power plants, are not reliable enough for SaaS. If you are in the Global North, you might have access to those resources but limited funding, which puts you in a similar boat. In this chapter I list approaches, given the circumstances at the time of writing; nevertheless, it is still a recommended path. SaaS is hitherto a more accessible business than biotech, medtech, or other approaches that require intensive experimentation, research, and development.

Building AI solutions with little investment

The lack of reliable electricity and internet connectivity hampers the ability to access cloud computing services. In rural areas in the Global South, where the majority of the population resides, the infrastructure required to support cloud computing is often inadequate or non-existent. This restricts access to cloud services, as the necessary infrastructure, such as data centers and high-speed internet connections, is not readily available.

Connectivity issues also pose a significant challenge. Africa has a relatively low internet penetration rate compared to other regions, and the available connections are often slow and unreliable. Limited bandwidth and frequent disruptions make it difficult for individuals and businesses to access cloud computing resources effectively. This lack of connectivity not only affects the ability to access cloud services but also impacts the overall user experience, resulting in slower data transfer speeds and increased latency.

Nevertheless, buying infrastructure is generally not recommended as it represents a considerable investment. Moreover, where servers are located raises a series of questions about the security of the data contained. With cloud computing, instead of using a physical hard drive, cloud technology enables us to access and store data via the internet. In practice, we

155

upload data and software into a remote server, and we grant users the use of those services remotely.

Amazon Web Service is currently the major worldwide provider. Interestingly, they have computational resources also located in the Global South (including Jakarta, Rio de Janeiro, and Cape Town). If you operate in the Global South, it is advised that you choose a machine located closer to you to avoid lags, and from reliable providers. Regarding what to upload as your service, there are plenty of tools nowadays to accelerate their creation and deployment. Those now even include integration to pre-trained AI models.

There is a growing landscape of large language models (LLMs). Given the pace of innovation of the field, it is not worth describing them in detail here as they will quickly become obsolete, hence, I am only going to describe the fundamental principles. Moreover, this is not a purely technical text (in case of interest, I recommend you read the referenced text). LLMs are a type of AI algorithm related to the human language. They utilize deep-learning techniques and massive data sets to process and generate human-like text. These models are characterized by their extensive size, which is made possible by the use of AI accelerators (specialized hardware that can handle vast amounts of data). LLMs can perform various natural language processing tasks, such as recognizing, summarizing, translating, predicting, and generating content.[114] They are trained through deep-learning algorithms and have the ability to understand and generate text in a manner similar to the human language.[115] These models have gained significant attention and popularity in recent years due to their potential applications in fields like text generation, chatbots, and language translation. By leveraging massive amounts of data and complex algorithms, LLMs have the potential to greatly enhance our ability to interact with and understand natural language.

There are similarly many models trained to detect objects in images. Some are instead aimed at generating data, given some text input or original images as a starting point.[116] At the basis of these, there are convolutional neural networks, a type of deep-learning architecture, which are commonly used for AI image processing. Those networks automatically learn and extract hierarchical features from images. They consist of layers with optimized filters to respond to specific patterns, like edges, textures, and more complex features, to ultimately classify an object represented in the picture.

Ukheshe Technologies

Ukheshe in Zulu means cash. Ukheshe Technologies is a South African-founded fintech company that has made a significant impact on financial inclusion in South Africa.[117] The company was developed in 2018 as a digital platform to address and improve financial inclusion within the country. Ukheshe's CEO and cofounder, Clayton Hayward, emphasizes the role of technology in enabling financial inclusion for Africa in general.

The innovation

- Ukheshe Technologies' flagship product is Eclipse API, an interoperable digital transaction platform. IT enables customers to accept, move, and distribute digital currency and virtual card payment solutions.

- The platform can integrate with national payment switches, banks, and mobile money wallets. It is an SaaS hosted on Amazon Web Services (AWS). Its architecture is based on tools such as Kafka, Dockers, and Angular, and databases based on MySQL and MongoDB.

Challenges faced

- The major challenges come from information security and cyberattacks.

- Ukheshe Technologies is currently working on addressing the growing concerns around information security and protecting their systems and data from potential cyberattacks.

Business model and success factors

- Ukheshe is primarily a B2B company (the company sells its transaction platform and solutions to partners). Revenue comes from volume-based transaction fees and monthly subscription fees. Over sixty enterprise partners include major banks, telecoms, and retailers in South Africa.

- Fintech represents a growing market, especially in Africa.

Impact

- Over 100 million digital transactions processed, worth over USD$130 million as of 2020.
- During COVID-19 lockdowns, Ukheshe helped governments distribute social welfare grants to citizens through mobile payments.
- It provides financial access to large unbanked, underserved populations across Africa.
- They won awards for innovation and advancing digital payments in Africa.

Key takeaways

- Ukheshe built an interoperable digital payments ecosystem for Africa. Its micropayment solutions enable financial inclusion of the unbanked people.
- Its significant social impact is represented by providing digital transaction access and enabling development at a different level.

Unleashing the power of SaaS and their limitations

Apart the aforementioned issues related to infrastructure, sometimes SaaS companies have additional problems. For instance, some SaaS products collect payments through third-party platforms such as Stripe, which are not available in certain countries for security reasons. Therefore, in practice, the company has the additional step of legally registering the company in another country, which is considered to be safer. The moment you perform the secondary registration, you might encounter further taxes or even double taxation, which can dramatically hamper your revenue. For instance, fewer people will trust a company registered in Nigeria, and registering a company in the US as a non-US citizen will create further hurdles.

Nevertheless, one of the advantages of SaaS products is that customers can be anywhere in the world, as long as they have access to the internet. Decentralization of customers comes at a huge benefit.

Moreover, despite the decentralization, further regulatory challenges might be related to the residence of the users. In Europe we have data privacy regulations like General Data Protection Regulation (GDPR); in California there is the California Consumer Privacy Act (CCPA). To comply with regulations on data subject consent—the right to access and erase personal information—and data breach notifications, SaaS vendors must establish correct data-handling practices. SaaS companies confront increased difficulty in managing compliance across geographical boundaries as more nations enact privacy legislation. With cloud-based systems, it might be challenging to follow different data residency and cross-border transfer regulations.

In accordance with industry standards like ISO 27001, SaaS companies must also have rigorous cybersecurity procedures in place. SaaS apps are a prime target for hackers since they store data centrally rather than locally. Data loss and illegal access must be avoided at all costs. Neglecting to protect sensitive information may constitute a privacy violation and damage client confidence.

SaaS companies must also adhere to standards that are often specific to certain businesses, such as the Health Insurance Portability and Accountability Act (HIPAA) for the healthcare sector. Before utilizing SaaS platforms, customers need guarantees that they adhere to relevant compliance standards. To meet industry standards, vendors must validate security, availability, integrity, and other measures. It is generally recommended to startups based on SaaS businesses to stay vigilant to new and possibly conflicting regulations that might appear or relate to specific geographical regions, despite the decentralized nature of an SaaS business.

Uipath

UiPath is a leading robotic process automation company, originally from Romania.[118] It was founded in Bucharest, Romania, in 2005 by Daniel Dines and Marius Tirca. The company develops software robots to automate repetitive and manual business processes. It raised over USD$1 billion in funding and has a valuation of USD$10.2 billion (as of April 2021).

The innovation

- UiPath proposes a series of solutions related to automation as a web interface for design workflow, and other tools for designing industrial robot manipulation processes, combining simplicity and connectivity.

Challenges faced

- Romania is suffering from relative political instability and high transaction costs (even for transaction exchanges into Euro). Corruption is still present at many levels.

- UiPath needed to open another office in New York, US, most likely to appear more reliable to investors.

Business model and success factors

- Software as a Service (SaaS)—UiPath do not produce the robots but the platform using them.

- UiPath uses the subscription model, with a free trial version of products to get users onboard and an advanced version with features and enterprise support.

- They rapidly expanded their global presence to have operations in over thirty countries.

- They built a network of implementation partners to gain new enterprise customers.

- They are focused on customer success and product innovation.

Impact

- Over 9,000 customers, including Starbucks, NASA, and HP.

- Clients achieved 70% to 90% cost savings on processes automated by UiPath.

Key takeaways

- UiPath has become a leader in helping companies leverage robotic process automation to improve efficiency.
- It has achieved hyper-growth through strong product-market fit and partnerships.
- UiPath was initially based in Romania, which is an attractive country for startup at the moment due to low taxes and low fixed costs, for instance related to rent. Yet, most likely to be more reliable to investors, they moved their headquarters to New York, US. This is a common case. In order to grow, often a company will need to relocate so it can scale up investors.
- Both Romania and South Africa were not considered as startup or innovation hubs, like Silicon Valley, London, or other tech places. Yet, we managed to see that some interesting case studies exist.

Accessing quantum computing

Whether quantum computing will be the next revolution is unclear, despite the initial hype. We have so far experienced little improvement, though this can be related to the fact that the technology is relatively young.

In layman terms, quantum computing takes advantage of the quantum physics phenomena to perform computations in fundamentally different ways from classical computing.[119] Qubits are the basic units of information, which can exist as one, zero, or a super-position of both states simultaneously due to quantum uncertainty. This contradicts the current computing paradigm where bits are clearly either zero or one. This fundamental difference has been explored in terms of logic gates or taking advantages or other quantum phenomena, such as the quantum tunneling, to achieve better optimizations.

Quantum computers currently require costly hardware and a multitude of researchers improving them. From the perspective of low resources, it is unimaginable that someone will build a quantum computer in his or her garage at a low cost. Nevertheless, some quantum computers are currently accessible as cloud services.

Currently there are different approaches, though the main trends are represented by the IBM Quantum computer (and the associated Qiskit library)[120] and quantum annealers such as D-Wave.[121] Quantum computing and quantum annealing are two different approaches to harnessing the power of quantum mechanics for solving computational problems. Qiskit and D-Wave are platforms that represent these two approaches, respectively. Both of them have a Python implementation.

Qiskit is an open-source library and abstract circuits designer developed by IBM. It is intended for general-purpose quantum computing, which uses quantum gates to manipulate quantum bits (qubits) to perform computations. Similar to conventional logic gates, quantum gates work with qubits' quantum state, which can be in a superposition of several states at once. Users can build, model, and run quantum circuits using Qiskit's tools and libraries on a variety of backends, including accessible quantum hardware.

In quantum annealing, the system begins in a straightforward initial state and develops toward the ground state of an energy function unique to the issue. The objective is to identify the qubit configuration that minimizes this energy function, which is equivalent to the best answer to the optimization issue. This strategy works especially well for combinatorial optimization issues when the goal is to choose the optimum configuration from a wide range of options. The D-Wave 2X and D-Wave Advantage systems are specialized quantum annealers created to carry out this annealing procedure for optimization issues.

The essential methods for applying quantum physics to computation are what distinguish Qiskit (quantum computing) from D-Wave (quantum annealing). While D-Wave focuses on quantum annealing to address optimization issues, Qiskit focuses on general-purpose quantum computing employing quantum gates and circuits. Both strategies can possibly address various kinds of computing issues, but each has its own advantages and disadvantages.

Nevertheless, for low-resource settings, the idea is the same as traditional SaaS, in the sense that those quantum computers provide you with a service accessible remotely through internet connection. You need to learn the programming language, access it through some kind of console, and use it through a normal cloud. It is not impossible to imagine that someone could build further SaaS businesses connecting to the quantum computers, as it is currently happening with the more common Amazon Web Services. If you are in Zimbabwe, Jakarta or Pizzo Calabro, you do not need to buy a quantum computer; you only need an internet connection.

Biotech and medtech

SaaS is probably the main approach for startup. However, new technologies such as machine learning and telecommunication have become pervasive in other domains. Consider the big data available from genomics, medical imaging, and clinical biomarkers. Indeed those are niches: biotech, medical imaging, neurotech. In some cases it is difficult to give advice about how to access affordable technologies in those contexts as they actually have high entry barriers: expensive devices, antibodies, or other chemical reagents. From the computational perspective, having access to specific databases is critical, as having the digitized version of each sample with biological information is more practical and affordable than handling the tangible biological specimen. Luckily, some resources are available, and more comprehensive references are given in the Further Reading section. Research databases: online platforms like GenBank, UCSC Genome Browser, and Ensembl provide extensive databases of genomic information, including DNA sequences, gene annotations, and genetic variations. These databases are valuable for researchers to access and analyze genomic data. Genomic data repositories: publicly available data repositories such as the National Center for Biotechnology Information (NCBI) and European Molecular Biology Laboratory's European Bioinformatics Institute (EMBL-EBI) house vast collections of genomic data, including complete genomes, transcriptomes, and epigenomes. These repositories allow researchers to access and analyze large-scale genomic datasets. Imaging repository for diseases are also available, such as the Alzheimer Disease Neuro Imaging Initiative (ADNI), Parkinson's Progression Markers Initiative (PPMI), and the Center for Biomedical Research Excellence (COBRE) initiative for schizophrenia.

Sometimes some simple tools used in between the bio-specimen and IT infrastructure are unnecessarily expensive. For instance, a chamber for electrophoresis is just a plexiglass box with some electrodes. While I do not want to take responsibility for whether someone in a lab is doing experiments against legal or conventional protocol, it is true that there are possibilities to avoid extra costs.

Indeed, the figure of "bio-hacker" has emerged. This is not to be confused with influencers or YouTubers proposing pseudoscience vitamins. I am referring to communities like the HIVE in Ghana, the Waag Academy in the Netherlands, and the Mbaolab in Cameroon. These are learning spaces where people constantly try affordable ways to perform expensive biotech experiments. Reverse-engineering devices or simple tools that are no longer under patents can be made accessible as open-source hardware. Notable famous cases are the CRISPR/Cas9 do it yourself kit from Josiah Zayner,[122] and the homemade COVID-19 vaccine from Professor George Church from the Wyss Institute.[123] (Although, these last two are probably highly controversial figures, and I do not want to lose ourselves debating them.)

Instead, I would like to mention Eva Harris. She is a professor of infectious diseases and vaccinology at the University of Berkeley, US. She is also the director of the Sustainable Sciences Institute (SSI),[124] a non-profit organization founded by her in 1998 in Nicaragua. Harris arrived in Nicaragua for the first time in 1988 as a volunteer for a humanitarian organization. After a decade of almost financial survivalism, she managed to establish a laboratory carrying out top-notch diagnostics and research with limited access. Reading her texts and papers, it is possible to see the feasibility of having a research lab with almost no resources. For instance, we can learn how to perform polymerase chain reactions, which have been particularly known after the COVID-19 pandemic, with rudimental resources.[125] Moreover, the SSI has also contributed to research related to Zika, Dengue, and Chikungunya diseases, as well as community capacity building in different underserved areas in Latin America. Their impact proves that it is possible to conduct research and development in biology, which is generally financially prohibitive with limited financial resources.

Summary

In this chapter we discussed how software as a service (SaaS) can be a viable business model for startups and innovation, even with limited resources. We outlined challenges like unreliable infrastructure and regulations but highlighted how SaaS allows the creation of services for users anywhere. Nevertheless, the general recommendation is to keep a lean approach and to build computationally efficient SaaS solutions. We also mentioned how emerging technologies like quantum computing and AI can be accessed through cloud platforms in an affordable manner. Finally, we acknowledged that biotech and medtech have higher barriers to entry, but options such as public databases, open-source hardware, and frugal innovation to do research with limited resources exist. In the end, through creativity and awareness of challenges, it is possible to achieve impactful innovation using all those technologies and modest financial inputs.

EIGHT

Fostering A Sustainable Future

The industrial revolution sparked a series of innovations that led us to where we are today. This bulge of factories, engineering, workers, production, and distribution brought us all benefits and increased the quality of life that we enjoy every day. Unfortunately, it also led to levels of carbon emissions that in recent years have become seriously concerning. What until now has been contributing to improve our lives is threatening to destroy them. Negative effects of global warming include: reducing crop yields due to higher temperatures, more frequent and intense hurricanes, more frequent droughts and floods, increased air pollution, and consequently more chronic diseases. Due to disrupted economies, we might experience more famine and therefore more forced migrations.

These effects unfortunately are expected to increase each year.

We already have all the tools and technologies to address this, as have been studied and documented, where with proper employment of solar, wind, and other renewable energy innovations, we could address all current energy needs.[126] However, as mentioned in Chapter 4, barriers for adoption exist, or conservativism and lobbying at high levels might delay this.

Nevertheless, some scholars suggest that due to the constant increase of energy demands from computational innovations, new technologies, and increasing populations, even all the possible renewable energy solutions will never be able to address the needs.[127] In this view, environmental sustainability and the economy are incompatible, and despite false promises of possible decoupling between economic growth and pollution,[128] the only possible option could be an economic degrowth. Economic degrowth proposes a deliberate reduction in economic activity and resource consumption to achieve a more sustainable and equitable society. The main idea behind economic degrowth is to shift from a focus on material accumulation and GDP growth toward ensuring the well-being of both humans and the planet. Being realistic, not many governments are willing or in a condition to actuate a degrowth on a large scale, therefore we are back into our bottom-up approach, entrusting witty individuals to find solutions among all these constraints.

Impact and current damages

Everyone loves ChatGPT and other chatbots able to produce seamless long text with perfect grammar, using the human language. However, few people are aware of the severe environmental harm that has been caused by these. If we take into consideration ChatGPT-3, its language model needed to be trained extensively, which required the use of a computer, which required power, resulting in 502 tons of CO_2 used to produce the necessary electricity. According to Stanford University research on the AI Index, this is roughly comparable to 600 flights every week between New York and San Francisco.[129]

A single ChatGPT prompt seems to spend 100 times as much energy as a single Google search, which is surprising given how much energy LLM training requires. Each prompt consumes 0.3 kWh per request as opposed to 0.0003 kWh per Google search. These figures appear insignificant, but when it comes to energy costs and environmental effects, they represent the ratio of 1:1000 for one ChatGPT search and a thousand Google searches. Considering how many users there are in the entire world, if they all use ChatGPT and not Google we have an idea how severe the increase in the carbon footprint could be.

Additionally, this is only considering ChatGPT; alternative models or AWS services are not more environmentally friendly. The infrastructure that underpins AI, such as data centers, cloud networks, and edge devices, consumes a lot of energy and resources and therefore contributes to the emission of thousands of dangerous chemical compounds. The energy consumption of AI is a critical concern due to the exponential growth of data and the necessity for ever-more-powerful computer resources with the building of ever-larger neural networks or LLMs.

In terms of carbon emissions and the materials required to build and maintain the necessary infrastructure, AI has high energy requirements. The serious negative environmental implications of AI have been highlighted in numerous studies that have looked at the carbon footprint of this technology. Emma Strubell and colleagues presented at the Thirty-Fourth AAAI Conference on Artificial Intelligence in 2020, a paper titled "Energy and Policy Considerations for Modern Deep-Learning Research." In the manuscript, the authors assert that training a single deep-learning model can result in up to 284,000 kg of CO_2, which is similar to the energy consumption of five cars over the course of their lifetime.[130] Moreover, Strubell and colleagues pointed out that the bottleneck is hyperparameters tuning, and an alternative to a brute-force grid search should be introduced, such as a Bayesian hyper-parameters search. However, currently most trained models disregard this advice.

The carbon footprint of electricity is not the only issue. We need increasingly powerful computational cards that must be continually updated to train AI models. But what happens to the older ones? While some used computational cards are resold, the majority are turned into e-waste,[131] where dangerous pollutants are prevalent. In the rest of the chapter, I revise some general ideas related to the green economy, then we will delve into more technical solutions related to decreasing the computational expenses of training AI models.

Green economy

The term "green economy" mostly refers to the focus of commercial ventures in lessening environmental damage, and in increasing climate change resilience. This requires a broad shift toward sustainability across all industries. Variations of this include the circular economy, doughnut economy, and other frameworks for sustainable development. The main goal is to promote innovation, job development, and more fair growth, while providing a comprehensive vision and doable solutions to prevent a climate catastrophe.[132] In some contexts, this is referred to as "decoupling," as we need to have a disassociation between utility profits and energy consumption.

Some changes are already ongoing. Renewable energy is rapidly growing as a result of solar and wind energy's steep price declines. One example of an energy-efficient technology that is gaining popularity is light-emitting diode lighting. As battery prices decrease, the market for electric vehicles is also booming. The principles of the circular economy that aim to cut waste are being adopted. Corporate strategies and investor objectives are becoming increasingly sustainable. However, the rate and scope of change must sharply increase. Many governments around the world still strongly support fossil fuels' usage and have not yet tightened their environmental laws.

In our bottom-up approach, we have to focus on how businesses must continue improving efficiency, developing green products and services, and fully integrating sustainability into their operations. Investors should assess climate risks and opportunities of ventures before investing, as in the future, non-sustainable companies might be taxed.

A just transition is crucial for public and political buy-in. With vision, collaboration, and commitment, a thriving green economy that delivers prosperity while healing the planet is within reach. The technological and entrepreneurial foundations are firmly in place. What is needed now is decisive leadership and financing to activate the transformation. By pioneering the green economy, we can set the stage for a sustainable future. Fortunately, renewable energy investment is on the rise, with big companies like Google and Apple, as well as small firms, installing solar panels on their roofs. By doing this, we hope that carbon emissions and reliance on fossil fuels will be reduced.

There are even companies explicitly focused on environmental issues:

- **Beyond Meat**[133] is a company producing plant-based meat alternatives, capitalizing on consumer interest in reducing meat consumption due to the huge carbon footprint of animal agriculture. Its valuation has skyrocketed recently, as it promises to disrupt the meat industry.

- **SolarCity**[134]—now a subsidiary of Tesla—installs solar panels on homes and businesses, profiting from the demand for distributed renewable energy. Many new solar companies are competing in this space.

For the rest of the chapter we describe another company explicitly focused on the green economy, and then we close the loop by discussing the green approach to reduce energy consumption in the context of SaaS and AI solutions.

Ecovative Design LLC

Ecovative Design LLC was founded in 2007 in Green Island, US, by Eben Bayer and Gavin McIntyre. They developed mushroom-based packaging and building materials as eco-friendly alternatives. Despite their exotic idea, they raised over USD$60 million in funding from investors like IKEA and 3M.[135]

The innovation

- Leverages mycelium, the root structure of mushrooms, as a renewable and compostable material.

- Invented proprietary technology to grow mycelium into different shapes and consistencies.

- Enables tuning of properties like density, rigidity, and acoustic absorption.

- The produced material can be used as protective packaging, used by Dell, IKEA, and others; or as a leather alternative, used by companies like Bolt Threads.

Challenges faced

- To achieve comparable products for packaging like Styrofoam required some research and development, especially where digital fabrication was required.

- To remain cost-competitive, they needed to define a process for growing the mycelium that was not too expensive.

Business model and success factors

- A B2B revenue model producing materials for brands based on partnerships and contracts.

- Positioned as a sustainable solution relative to traditional plastics and foams.

Impact

- Materials decompose fully in sixty to ninety days with no microplastics remaining, as opposed to

Styrofoam, which represents a hazard from an environmental point of view.

- Reduced landfill waste and carbon emissions relative to conventional packaging by using Ecovative products.

Key takeaways

- Ecovative pioneered innovative biomaterials from mycelium as eco-friendly alternatives.
- They enabled brands to adopt more sustainable practices around packaging and materials.
- The company created rapid revenue growth and strong market potential in a green materials space.

Environmentally friendly IT solutions

The possibilities where the AI sector must decrease its carbon footprint are related to energy-efficient hardware design and renewable energy options. Energy-efficient hardware includes cards with graphical processor units, which significantly reduce the energy required to run AI applications, decreasing the impact on the environment, for example, neuromorphic hardware[136] and programmable resistors.[137] "Sparse" neural networks can use those approaches while training that use a smaller amount of connections between neurons and the computational load, because we are only training a portion of the model and reusing older ones. Transfer learning and federated learning can also help lower our carbon footprint. As there are difficulties in developing models for medical imaging that are related to energy efficiency, there are currently activities to put ideas into practice.[138] Indeed, low-rank adaptation during transfer learning can heavily reduce the number of trainable parameters without sacrificing performance.

Better models ought to be applied. Several researchers are aiming to create language models using data sets that are 1/10,000 the size of the enormous language models (like a part of language a child can have compared to an adult). For example, the BabyLM Challenge[139] aims at teaching a language model how to learn linguistic nuances naturally from scratch using a dataset of the words that young infants are exposed to. For the BabyLM Challenge, the dataset's maximum word count is 100,000, or roughly the number of words a thirteen-year-old child will have heard. Young children hear between 2,000 and 7,000 words each year. Because it is simpler to train and utilizes less time and resources, a smaller model consumes less energy.

Smart meters are devices that track electricity usage and report it to the utility companies. The quantity of energy used by a household is measured and recorded, and the consumer is informed of their energy costs via an in-home display. Based on the analysis of multiple studies, there is evidence to suggest that the use of electricity smart meters leads to better energy management.[140] Among the advantages, they allow data analytics that can be utilized to identify customers who respond positively to energy management initiatives, such as dynamic pricing, enabling targeted interventions, and improved energy efficiency.[141]

From the success of smart meters, computational smart meters have been introduced. I am not referring to machine-learning-based smart meters, but in gauging the training of the machine-learning model during their training. Those are generally Python libraries converting the central and graphics processor units usage into energy consumption, ultimately estimating the carbon emissions and taking into account the regional emission coefficient.[142] In this way, a user can be aware of how much training is responsible for carbon emission, and can decide whether to take action.

Lastly, more energy-efficient cooling systems should be used, as cooling systems in some cases use considerable amounts of energy. It is generally difficult to appropriately cool data centers using traditional cooling methods like air or hydraulic conditioning. The usage of a more energy-efficient cooling system should be considered, for example, Microsoft is testing a totally underwater cooling system.[143]

Sustainable AI is more than just a passing fad; it is a long-term approach to developing AI systems that can meet present needs without representing a threat to future generations to meet their own. As we continue to rely on AI to solve complex problems and foster innovation, it is critical that we adopt a long-term perspective that takes into account the social, economic, and environmental implications of our actions. Sustainable means long term, and we need a fundamental shift in how we think about innovation if we are to have long-term strategy. We must place greater emphasis on sustainable problem solving and design thinking over specialized technological improvements.

Waiting for this cultural shift to arrive, to create AI systems that are truly sustainable from an environmental, social, and technological point of view for our future generations, we need to work with specialists from a number of disciplines, including environmental science, social science, engineering, and computer science. Through this collaboration, it may be possible to develop AI systems that are both sustainable and deeply cognizant of the complex social and environmental issues they are supposed to address.

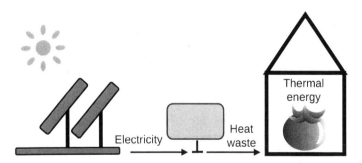

Idealization of a system using the heat waste from computer clusters as thermal energy for greenhouses

Heat waste: From chimneys to tomatoes

The human mind is limitless. Kamil Brejcha is a Czech software developer and cofounder of the digital trading platform Nakamotox. For the love of nature (and less of AI), in 2018 Kamil created a peculiar greenhouse for his tomatoes, put together from hydroponics, solar power, cryptocurrency mining, recycled water, sensors, and Internet of Things. In practice, he created a rudimental greenhouse by himself with the heat to nurture the tomatoes coming straight from the heat waste of the computers he was using for bitcoin mining.[144] Depending on the geographic location, greenhouses need additional heating to withstand cold winters, and this obviously requires energy, while computers, on top of using electricity to run, need cooling and produce heat waste. By using the heat waste of computer clusters inside a greenhouse, two problems are solved at the same time: the need for heating the greenhouse and the need for cooling the computers.

Indeed, cryptocurrency mining has been pointed out as another major catastrophe for the environment as it is a huge waste of energy that creates a lot of heat.[145] A single special purpose computer generates heat at a temperature of 35–40°C. According to current estimates, computers utilize 61,230 Gigawatt hours of electricity annually. Additionally, computers generate a lot of heat waste that necessitates constant air conditioning, resulting in additional energy waste.

On the other hand, many locations throughout the world have inadequate heating systems that are to blame for the production of a significant amount of hazardous fumes. Numerous researchers have examined the economic viability of heat waste recovery techniques in greenhouses, similar to those depicted in the figure above. Overall, it has been determined that heat waste is advantageous for greenhouses, if used properly, particularly in the winter and in northern regions as heating expenses account for a significant amount of greenhouse expenses.[146] Although this sounds absurd, a few businesses in Canada, Finland, and Singapore are considering the solution. Mint-Green, a Canadian cleantech cryptocurrency miner, came up with the absurd concept of converting more than 96% of the electricity consumed for bitcoin mining into heat energy using digital boilers.[147] Due to the fact that cryptocurrency mining machines are constantly operating at full capacity, there is a rare chance to offer a dependable, eco-friendly heating baseload for North Vancouver's district energy system. In fact, the city of Vancouver will integrate a cutting-edge heat source into its district energy system in 2022 that is based on bitcoin mining. Compared to natural gas, the goal is to stop 20,000 tons of greenhouse gases from entering the atmosphere. This strategy claims that producing both usable thermal energy and bitcoin is a successful way to develop low-carbon heating technologies.

Another Canadian mining firm, Heatmine, operates in Quebec, on the other side of the country. Quebec is a relatively forward-thinking region where the majority of its electricity is generated from renewable sources. However, the corporation realized that by collecting the leftover heat from its mining machines, it could also increase the value of that electricity. In 2018, Heatmine installed fifteen units, which were dispersed among greenhouses, a private residence, and multiple warehouses.[148] To my knowledge, despite the project's initial success, it now appears to have completely collapsed and the company has dissolved.

I wanted to close this chapter with a negative outcome example. This is a reminder that it is great to have revolutionary ideas, and we need them, especially in the sustainable development context. However, it is worth reminding ourselves that the market is the judge, and sometimes social and economic change is difficult. Failure is part of the game. Do not forget what we discussed so far, especially the validation of a product-market fit.

Summary

AI systems like ChatGPT—while impressive—have massive carbon footprints due to their energy-intensive training processes. This is because training models produce tons of CO_2 emissions. Proposed solutions include using smaller training datasets and energy-efficient hardware like neuromorphic chips, renewable energy, and collaboration across disciplines.

While creative ideas exist, economic viability remains a hurdle. Overall, in this chapter we argued that AI must become more sustainable through technical improvements like sparse neural networks as well as larger systemic changes toward a green economy and long-term thinking.

Conclusion

N ew social order and universal health coverage are expressions we hear quite frequently. Each person has the moral right (or duty) to contribute to his society, aiming for both and hopefully without falling into traps of utopian dynamics and false promises. In this book we discussed strategies for activists, entre- preneurs, and innovators to create positive change and prosperity, even in challenging environments with limited resources. Innovation plays a critical role in those circumstances. We emphasize a bottom-up approach driven by individuals rather than top-down government policies. This can be motivated by noble purposes, such as "wanting to change the world" or by the desire to create a venture, despite living in dif- ficult contexts or low-resource situations. Travel and see; words are just words—they cannot compare to first-person experiences, smells, and colors.

By now you should understand the importance of identifying pressing social or economic issues before seeking solutions. We should at this point know several methods for recognizing unmet needs, such as directly observing challenges people face, analyzing complaints in online forums, or finding weaknesses in existing businesses. Once a significant problem is identified, potential solutions can be devised. Creative capacity building and design thinking methodologies are recommended to foster innovation. These human-centered techniques aim to empower regular people to develop their own solutions to local problems. When implementing solutions, cooperating with local stakeholders according to community customs and traditions is advised, especially in rural areas. In this book I summarized an example of obtaining approval from village chiefs before launching projects in their communities. Although you won't necessarily have this same need, I hope it helps you realize the multi-faceted reality of this world.

For entrepreneurs, tips were provided on finding aligned cofounders, protecting intellectual property strategically, acquiring initial customers, and quickly launching products to get market feedback. Building trust and credibility is also crucial when introducing a new brand. Choosing the right business model is a key decision. In terms of technology, leveraging affordable digital tools like SaaS, low-code platforms, and public data sets can help innovators with limited resources. Quantum computing, AI, and biotech offer promising capabilities but also have challenges regarding their access, skills, and infrastructure if you do not live in high-income countries or have limited budget.

Running sustainable projects and considering environmental impact is vital. High resource consumption and carbon emissions are associated with modern technology, emphasizing the need for green solutions. My hope is to offer practical advice and case studies for change-makers aiming to create a positive impact in society, even when faced with systemic constraints. I advocate for a bottom-up, human-centric approach focused on real needs and continuous improvement. In all this, it is critical that we live in a context of peace—war and conflicts are the main disturbance to development.

We started with a high-level question: "What is wealth?" Now I would like to close with another high-level question: "Why do we want to change the world?" This is probably a big assumption, as not everybody reading this text has this exaggerated goal (maybe you were simply looking for tips on how to start a business in your own challenging environment, although I imagine some readers could be motivated by achieving social justice or making our society a bit better). As we discussed, often the best way to reduce poverty is to create business. Therefore, involuntarily I imagine you are making the world a better place.

Just a reminder: being an entrepreneur or activist could be mentally and physically draining. Those who work to improve the world frequently invest their hearts and souls in the cause. While this passion is admirable, it's crucial to practice self-care to avoid burnout. I know it is hard, especially if it has become part of your lifestyle and even identity, but make time for rest, relaxation, and relationships beyond your mission. Realize that being a scientist, an activist, or a startup founder is just a job like any other. Therefore, connect with the parts of life that replenish you, whether this is time in nature, reading, exercising, or spending time with loved ones. We all need to eat well, get adequate sleep, and stay hydrated, otherwise if you start falling apart, then nobody will take care of your venture or organization. Take good care of yourself so you can continue to contribute to society.

Glossary

AI	Artificial intelligence
API	Application programming interface
B2B	Business to business
B2C	Business to customers
CCB	Creative Capacity Building
CCPA	California Consumer Privacy Act
CE	Conformité Européenne
CEO	Chief executive officer
EFLM TE-WG	Test Evaluation Working Group of the European Federation of Clinical Chemistry and Laboratory Medicine
EPO	European Patent Office
FDA	Food and Drug Administration

GDP   Gross domestic product

GDPR   General Data Protection Regulation

HDI   Human Development Index

HIPAA Health Insurance Portability and
Accountability Act

IPO   Initial Public Offering

LLM   Large language model

MIT   Massachusetts Institute of Technology

MRI   Magnetic resonance imaging

MVP   Minimum viable product

NGO   Non-governmental organization

PDI   Power distance index

QMS   Quality management system

SaaS   Software as a Service

SSI   Sustainable Sciences Institute

USD   United States Dollar

USPTO United States Patent and Trademark Office

VC   Venture Capital

References

1   World Bank Open Data, https://data.worldbank.org, accessed 16 November 2023

2   Akiwumi, P, *LDC Insight #3: Digitalization as a driver of structural transformation in African LDCs* (United Nations 2023), www.un.org/technologybank/news/digitalization-driver-structural-transformation-african-ldcs, accessed 16 November 2023

3   Pankhurst, R, "'Primitive money' in Ethiopia", *Journal des Africanistes*, 32/2 (1962), 213–248, https://persee.fr/doc/jafr_0037-9166_1962_num_32_2_1358, accessed 28 November 2023

4   Kurlansky, M, *Salt: A World History* (Jonathan Cape, 2003)

5   Beinhocker, ED, *The Origin Of Wealth: Evolution, complexity, and the radical remaking of economics* (Harvard Business Press, 2006)

6   The Organisation for Economic Cooperation and Development, "OEDC Health Statistics 2023", www.oecd.org/health/health-data.htm, accessed 8 October 2023

7   Schüssler, M, "The Gini is still in the bottle", *Moneyweb* (2014), https://moneyweb.co.za/archive/the-gini-is-still-in-the-bottle, accessed 21 November 2023

8   Stanton, EA, "The human development index: A history",
    Working Paper Series No. 127, *PERI Working Papers* (2007),
    https://doi.org/10.7275/1282621
9   The World Bank, "GDP (current US$) – Poland",
    https://data.worldbank.org/indicator/NY.GDP.MKTP.
    CD?locations=PL, accessed 8 October 2023
10 The World Bank, "GDP growth (annual %) – Singapore",
    https://data.worldbank.org/indicator/NY.GDP.MKTP.
    KD.ZG?locations=SG, accessed 8 October 2023
11 Zalas-Kamiñska, K, "Successful transformation—is it
    really something that Poland can give as an example to
    less developed countries?", *Development and Democracy*
    (2014), 152
12 Siddiqi, A and Hertzman, C, "Economic growth, income
    equality, and population health among the Asian Tigers",
    International Journal of Health Services, 31/2 (2001), 323–333,
    https://doi.org/10.2190/YFXB-E27P-HQDQ-04AM
13 Our World in Data, www.ourworldindata.org, accessed
    28 November 2023
14 Ashton, TS, *The Industrial Revolution, 1760–1830* (OUP
    Catalogue, 1997)
15 Acemoglu, D and Robinson, JA, *Why Nations Fail:
    The origins of power, prosperity and poverty* (Profile, 2012)
16 OpenStreetMap, https://openstreetmap.org, accessed
    28 November 2023
17 Centers for Medicare & Medicaid Services, *Medicare-
    Medicaid Enrollee State Profile: Arizona*, www.cms.gov/
    Medicare-Medicaid-Coordination/Medicare-and-
    Medicaid-Coordination/Medicare-Medicaid-Coordination-
    Office/Downloads/2007StateProfilesAZ.pdf, accessed
    8 October 2023
18 Arzaluz Solano, S and Jurado Montelongo, MA,
    "Estrategias de combate a la pobreza. El Programa Hábitat
    en ciudades fronterizas del norte de México: Los casos de
    Nogales, Sonora y Ciudad Juárez, Chihuahua", *Región y
    sociedad*, 18/37 (2006), 85–126
19 Sanderson, A, Thomas, L and Tafirenyika, M, "Factors
    affecting gold production in Zimbabwe (1980–2018)",
    Resources Policy, 73 (2021), https://doi.org/10.1016/j.
    resourpol.2021.102174
20 Sachs, JD and Warner, AM, "The big push, natural resource
    booms and growth", *Journal of Development Economics*,

59/1 (1999), 43–76, https://doi.org/10.1016/S0304-3878(99)00005-X

21 Weinthal, E and Jones Luong, P, "Combating the resource curse: An alternative solution to managing mineral wealth", *Perspectives on Politics*, 4/1 (March 2006), 35–53, https://doi.org/10.1017/S1537592706060051

22 Porter, ME, Stern, S and Green, M, *Social Progress Index 2014: Executive summary* (Social Progress Imperative, 2014), www.socialprogress.org/static/8ae51e47705a43b4db48be8 1856b8432/2014-social-progress-index-exec-summary.pdf, accessed 15 January 2024

23 Hofstede, G, "Dimensionalizing cultures: The Hofstede model in context", *Online Readings in Psychology and Culture*, 2/1 (2011), https://doi.org/10.9707/2307-0919.1014

24 Battistella, C, et al., "The impact of cultural dimensions on project management performance", *International Journal of Organizational Analysis*, 32/1 (2023), 108–130, https://doi.org/10.1108/IJOA-11-2022-3498

25 Basabe, N and Ros, M, "Cultural dimensions and social behavior correlates: Individualism-collectivism and power distance", *International Review of Social Psychology*, 18/1 (2005), 189–225

26 Kraay, A and McKenzie, D, "Do poverty traps exist? Assessing the evidence", *Journal of Economic Perspectives*, 28/3 (2014), 127–148, https://doi.org/10.1257/jep.28.3.127

27 Azariadis, C and Stachurski, J, "Poverty traps", *Handbook of Economic Growth*, 1 (2005), 295–384, https://doi.org/10.1016/S1574-0684(05)01005-1

28 Ngonghala, CN, et al., "General ecological models for human subsistence, health and poverty", *Nature Ecology & Evolution*, 1/8 (2017), 1153–1159, https://doi.org/10.1038/s41559-017-0221-8

29 Sachs, JD, *The End of Poverty: Economic possibilities for our time* (Penguin, 2006)

30 Moyo, D, *Dead Aid: Why aid is not working and how there is a better way for Africa* (Macmillan, 2009)

31 Easterly, W, *The Tyranny of Experts: Economists, dictators, and the forgotten rights of the poor* (Basic Books, 2014)

32 Elsenbroich, C, "The Addio Pizzo movement: Exploring social change using agent-based modelling", *Trends in Organized Crime*, 20 (2017), 120–138, https://doi.org/10.1007/s12117-016-9288-x

33   Banerjee, AV and Duflo, E, *Poor Economics: A radical rethinking of the way to fight global poverty* (PublicAffairs, 2012)

34   Ulrichs, M and Roelen, K, "Equal opportunities for all?– A critical analysis of Mexico's *Oportunidades*", *IDS Working Papers*, 1/23 (2012), https://doi.org/10.1111/j.2040-0209.2012.00413.x

35   Millett, P, *The Worst Form of Government* (Foreign, Commonwealth & Development Office, 2014), https://blogs.fcdo.gov.uk/petermillett/2014/03/05/the-worst-form-of-government, accessed 28 November 2023

36   Camerer, C, "Behavioral economics: Reunifying psychology and economics", *Proceedings of the National Academy of Sciences*, 96/19 (1999), 10575–10577, http://dx.doi.org/10.1073/pnas.96.19.10575

37   Duflo, E, "Scaling Up and Evaluation", Annual World Bank Conference on Development Economics (World Bank and OUP, 2004), 241–269

38   Beinhocker, ED, *The Origin of Wealth: Evolution, complexity, and the radical remaking of economics* (Harvard Business Press, 2006)

39   Ridley, M, *The Evolution of Everything: How new ideas emerge* (Harper, 2015)

40   Stokes, LC, *Short Circuiting Policy: Interest groups and the battle over clean energy and climate policy in the American States* (Oxford University Press, 2020)

41   Bayrasli, E, *From the Other Side of the World: Extraordinary entrepreneurs, unlikely places* (Public Affairs, 2015)

42   Adam, T and de Savigny, D, "Systems thinking for strengthening health systems in LMICs: Need for a paradigm shift", *Health Policy and Planning*, 27/4 (2012), iv1–iv3, https://doi.org/10.1093/heapol/czs084

43   Energy Dome, https://energydome.com, accessed 8 October 2023

44   Manaresi, F, Menon, C and Santoleri, P, "Supporting innovative entrepreneurship: An evaluation of the Italian 'Start-up Act'", *Industrial and Corporate Change*, 30/6 (2021), 1591–1614, https://doi.org/10.1093/icc/dtab033

45   Tavanti, M, "The cultural dimensions of Italian leadership: Power distance, uncertainty avoidance and masculinity from an American perspective", *Leadership*, 8/3 (2012), 287–301, https://doi.org/10.1177/1742715012441876

46 Zhou, Y and Liu, Y, "The geography of poverty: Review and research prospects", *Journal of Rural Studies*, 93 (2022), 408–416, https://doi.org/10.1016/j.jrurstud.2019.01.008

47 Goldin, I, *The Pursuit of Development: Economic growth, social change and ideas* (Oxford University Press, 2016)

48 Christensen, CM, Baumann, H, Ruggles, R and Sadtler, TM, "Disruptive innovation for social change", *Harvard Business Review*, 84/12 (2006), 94, https://hbr.org/2006/12/disruptive-innovation-for-social-change, accessed 23 November 2023

49 Christensen, CM, Ojomo, E and Dillon, K, *The Prosperity Paradox: How innovation can lift nations out of poverty* (HarperCollins, 2019)

50 Goldin, I, *The Pursuit of Development: Economic growth, social change and ideas* (Oxford University Press, 2016)

51 Coe, NM and Lee, YS, "'We've learnt how to be local': The deepening territorial embeddedness of Samsung–Tesco in South Korea", *Journal of Economic Geography*, 13/2 (2013), 327–356, http://dx.doi.org/10.1093/jeg/lbs057

52 Lami, www.lami.world, accessed 8 October 2023

53 Edukoya, www.edukoya.com, accessed 8 October 2023

54 Njanja, A, "mPharma raises $35 million in round joined by Tinder co-founder's JAM fund, Bharti executive", *Tech Crunch*, https://techcrunch.com/2022/01/05/mpharma-raises-35million-in-round-participated-by-tinder-co-founders-jam-fund-bharti-executive, accessed 8 October 2023

55 MoringaConnect, https://moringaconnect.com, accessed 8 October 2023

56 Yesudhas, D, Ambuj, S and Gromiha, MM, "COVID-19 outbreak: History, mechanism, transmission, structural studies and therapeutics", *Infection*, 49 (2021), 199–213, https://doi.org/10.1007/s15010-020-01516-2

57 Yock, P, et al, *Biodesign: The Process of Innovating Medical Technologies* (Cambridge University Press, 2015)

58 Monaghan, PJ, et al., "Practical guide for identifying unmet clinical needs for biomarkers", *EJIFCC*, 29/2 (2018), 129–137, https://pubmed.ncbi.nlm.nih.gov/30050396, accessed 23 November 2023

59 Vreman, RA, et al., "Unmet medical need: An introduction to definitions and stakeholder perceptions", *Value Health*, 22/11 (2019), 1275–1282, https://doi.org/10.1016/j.jval.2019.07.007

60 Chaturvedi, J and Srinivas, G, "MedTech innovation using a structured biodesign process: Barriers and opportunities", *Karnataka Paediatric Journal*, 36/2 (2021), 106–112

61 Yock, P, et al, *Biodesign: The Process of Innovating Medical Technologies* (Cambridge University Press, 2015)

62 Ibid.

63 Sattel, G, "Innovative companies get their best ideas from academic research – Here's how they do it," *Harvard Business Review* (19 April 2016), https://hbr.org/2016/04/innovative-companies-get-their-best-ideas-from-academic-research-heres-how-they-do-it, accessed 23 November 2023

64 Kral, L, *Innovation for Social Change: How wildly successful nonprofits inspire and deliver results* (John Wiley & Sons, 2022)

65 Ferreira, B, Silva, W, Oliveira, E and Conte, T, "Designing personas with empathy map", *SEKE*, 152 (May 2015), http://dx.doi.org/10.18293/SEKE2015-152

66 Hamilton Helmer, W, *7 Powers: The foundations of business strategy* (Helmer, 2016)

67 Clary, S, "How Airbnb hacked Craigslist for viral growth", *Hackernoon* (8 July 2021), https://hackernoon.com/how-airbnb-hacked-craigslist-for-viral-growth-24l35eg, accessed 8 October 2023

68 Davis, T and Higgins, J, "A Blockbuster failure: How an outdated business model destroyed a giant", *Bankruptcy Case Studies*, chapter 11 (Spring 2013), https://ir.law.utk.edu/utk_studlawbankruptcy/11, accessed 28 November 2023

69 History of Information, "Nintendo's 'Virtual Boy,' the first mass-produced virtual reality game system", www.historyofinformation.com/detail.php?id=3637, accessed 8 October 2023

70 Kienitz, E, et al., "Targeted intervention to increase creative capacity and performance: A randomized controlled pilot study", *Thinking Skills and Creativity*, 13 (2014), 57–66, http://dx.doi.org/10.1016/j.tsc.2014.03.002

71 Twende, https://twende.or.tz, accessed 8 October 2023

72 IMDb, "MacGyver", www.imdb.com/title/tt0088559, accessed 8 October 2023

73 Kienitz, E, et al., "Targeted intervention to increase creative capacity and performance: A randomized controlled pilot study", *Thinking Skills and Creativity*, 13 (2014), 57–66, http://dx.doi.org/10.1016/j.tsc.2014.03.002

74 Nkonya, E, et al., "Impact of creative capacity building of local innovators and communities on income, welfare and attitudes in Uganda", *3IE Impact Evaluation Report*, 124 (2020), https://doi.org/10.23846/PW2IE124

75 Hopkins, R, *The Transition Companion: Making your community more resilient in uncertain times* (Green Books, 2011)

76 Centola, D, *Change: How to make big things happen* (Hachette UK, 2021)

77 Dietz, T, *Decisions for Sustainability: Facts and values* (Cambridge University Press, 2023)

78 Y Combinator Co-Founder Matching, www.ycombinator.com/cofounder-matching, accessed 9 October 2023

79 CoFoundersLab, https://cofounderslab.com, accessed 9 October 2023

80 Indie Hackers, https://indiehackers.com, accessed 23 November 2023

81 FoundersList, https://founderslist.com, accessed 9 October 2023

82 F6S, www.f6s.com, accessed 9 October 2023

83 Founders DAO, https://foundersdao.io, accessed 9 October 2023

84 Trends.vc, www.trends.vc, accessed 9 October 2023

85 SPARK, https://event.fourwaves.com/spark/pages, accessed 23 November 2023

86 Consortium for Advancement of MRI Education and Research in Africa, www.cameramriafrica.org, accessed 9 October 2023

87 Africa Open Science Hardware summit, https://africaosh.com, accessed 9 October 2023

88 Kumasi Hive, www.facebook.com/kumasihive, accessed 9 October 2023

89 Baym, NK, "Rethinking the music industry", *Popular Communication*, 8/3 (2010), 177–180, https://doi.org/10.1080/15405702.2010.493419

90 Coursea, "What is a go-to-market strategy? And how to create one" (2023), www.coursera.org/articles/go-to-market-strategy, accessed 22 December 2023

91 Crimi, A, "Technology transfer from Academia to medtech startup" (2023), www.youtube.com/watch?v=eGBhuac95fI, accessed 18 October 2023

92 Shontell, A, *The First 20 People to Sign Up for Facebook and How They Knew Zuckerberg Business Insider* (31 May 2011),

www.businessinsider.com/the-first-20-people-to-sign-up-for-facebook-2011-5, accessed 9 October 2023

93 Kickstartsidehustle.com, *How the MVPs of the Billon Dollar Businesses Got Their First 1,000 Customers*, https://kickstartsidehustle.com/a-billion-dollar-mvp, accessed 9 October 2023

94 Raz, G, "Dropbox: Drew Houston", *How I Built This with Guy Raz* (9 November 2020), www.npr.org/2020/11/06/932199300/dropbox-drew-houston, accessed 9 October 2023

95 Siu, E, "How Canva Grew From 1K to 10M Users Without Paid Advertising", Levelling Up wth Eric Siu (24 December 2016), https://youtu.be/oSXDdiScICQ, accessed 22 December 2023

96 Mahoney, JG, "China's rise as an advanced technological society and the rise of digital orientalism", *Journal of Chinese Political Science*, 28/1 (2023), 1–24, https://doi.org/10.1007/s11366-022-09817-z

97 Amoah, B, et al., "Boosting antenatal care attendance and number of hospital deliveries among pregnant women in rural communities: A community initiative in Ghana based on mobile phones applications and portable ultrasound scans", *BMC Pregnancy and Childbirth*, 16 (2016), 1–10, https://doi.org/10.1186/s12884-016-0888-x

98 Nowak, D and Jakubczyk, E, "The freeze-drying of foods—The characteristic of the process course and the effect of its parameters on the physical properties of food materials", *Foods*, 9/10 (2020), 1488, https://doi.org/10.3390/foods9101488

99 Lamptey, E and Serwaa, D, "The use of Zipline drones technology for COVID-19 samples transportation in Ghana", *HighTech and Innovation Journal*, 1/2 (2020), 67–71, https://doi.org/10.28991/HIJ-2020-01-02-03

100 Prahalad, CK, "Bottom of the pyramid as a source of breakthrough innovations", *Journal of Product Innovation Management*, 29/1 (2012), 6–12, https://doi.org/10.1111/j.1540-5885.2011.00874.x

101 Yunus, M, *Banker to the Poor: The story of the Grameen Bank* (Penguin Books India, 1998)

102 Kaur, M, "Rural marketing: A case study on Hindustan Unilever Limited", *International Journal of Applied Research & Studies*, 2/6 (2013)

103   Embrace Global, www.embraceglobal.org, accessed
      9 October 2023

104   Veit, D, et al., "Business models: An information systems
      research agenda", *Business & Information Systems
      Engineering*, 6/1 (2014), 45–53, http://dx.doi.org/10.1007/
      s12599-013-0308-y

105   Wikipedia, "Uniti (automobile)", https://en.wikipedia.
      org/wiki/Uniti_(automobile), accessed 9 October 2023

106   Glick, M and Ruetschlin, C, "Big tech acquisitions and the
      potential competition doctrine: The case of Facebook",
      Institute for New Economic Thinking Working Paper Series, 104
      (October 2019), https://doi.org/10.36687/inetwp104

107   Wade, J, "Google buys YouTube—and a ton of liability",
      Risk Management, 57/4 (May 2010), 24

108   Microsoft, "Microsoft acquires GitHub", https://news.
      microsoft.com/announcement/microsoft-acquires-github,
      accessed 17 November 2023

109   Paradromics, www.paradromics.com, accessed 9 October
      2023

110   Matovu, B, et al., "Translating medical device innovations
      to market—a Ugandan perspective", *BMC Research
      Notes*, 16/262 (2023), https://doi.org/10.1186/s13104-023-
      06541-6

111   EUR-Lex, "Document 32017R0745", http://data.europa.
      eu/eli/reg/2017/745/oj, accessed 27 November 2023

112   EUR-Lex, "Document 32017R0746", http://data.europa.
      eu/eli/reg/2017/746/oj, accessed 27 November 2023

113   EUR-Lex, "Document 32001L0083", http://data.europa.
      eu/eli/dir/2001/83/oj, accessed 27 November 2023

114   Manning, CD, "Human language understanding &
      reasoning", *Daedalus*, 151/2 (2022), 127–138, https://
      amacad.org/publication/human-language-understanding-
      reasoning, accessed 27 November 2023

115   Dan, J and Martin JH, *Speech and Language Processing: An
      introduction to natural language processing, computational
      linguistics, and speech recognition* (Prentice Hall Series in
      Artificial Intelligence, 2009)

116   Goodfellow, I, et al., "Generative adversarial nets",
      Advances in Neural Information Processing Systems, 27
      (10 June 2014), https://papers.nips.cc/paper_files/
      paper/2014/file/5ca3e9b122f61f8f06494c97b1afccf3-Paper.
      pdf, accessed 27 November 2023

117   Ukheshe, www.ukheshe.com, accessed 9 October 2023

118   UiPath, www.uipath.com, accessed 10 October 2023

119   Nielsen, MA and Chuang, IL, "Quantum computation and quantum information", *Physics Today*, 54/2 (2001), 60

120   Cross, A, "The IBM Q experience and QISKit open-source quantum computing software", APS March Meeting 2018, https://meetings.aps.org/Meeting/MAR18/Session/L58.3, accessed 27 November 2023

121   Boothby, K, Bunyk, P, Raymond, J and Roy, A, "Next-generation topology of D-Wave quantum processors", *arXiv*, https://doi.org/10.48550/arXiv.2003.00133

122   Guerrini, CJ, Spencer, GE and Zettler, PJ, "DIY CRISPR", *North Carolina Law Review*, 97 (6 January 2019), 1399, https://scholarship.law.unc.edu/cgi/viewcontent.cgi?article=6743&context=nclr, accessed 28 November 2023

123   Regalado, A, "Some scientists are taking a DIY coronavirus vaccine, and nobody knows if it's legal or if it works", *MIT Technology Review* (29 July 2020), https://technologyreview.com/2020/07/29/1005720/george-church-diy-coronavirus-vaccine, accessed 28 November 2023

124   Sustainable Sciences Institute, www.sustainablesciences.org, accessed 9 October 2023

125   Harris, E, *A Low-cost Approach to PCR: Appropriate transfer of biomolecular techniques* (Oxford University Press, 1998)

126   Jacobson, MZ, *No Miracles Needed: How today's technology can save our climate and clean our air* (Cambridge University Press, 2023)

127   Smil, V, *How the World Really Works: A scientist's guide to our past, present and future* (Penguin UK, 2022)

128   Vogel, J and Hickel, J, "Is green growth happening? An empirical analysis of achieved versus Paris-compliant CO2–GDP decoupling in high-income countries", *The Lancet Planetary Health*, 7/9 (September 2023), e759–e769, https://doi.org/10.1016/S2542-5196(23)00174-2

129   Stanford University Human-Centered Artificial Intelligence, *Artificial Intelligence Index Report 2023* (2023), https://aiindex.stanford.edu/wp-content/uploads/2023/04/HAI_AI-Index-Report_2023.pdf, accessed 27 November 2023

130   Strubell, E, Ganesh, A and McCallum, A, "Energy and policy considerations for modern deep learning research",

AAAI-20/IAAI-20/EAAI-20 Proceedings, 34/9 (2020), https://doi.org/10.1609/aaai.v34i09.7123

131   Perkins, DN, et al., "E-waste: A global hazard", *Annals of Global Health*, 80/4 (2014), 286–295, https://doi.org/10.1016/j.aogh.2014.10.001

132   Lavrinenko, O, et al., "The role of green economy in sustainable development (Case study: The EU states)", *Journal of Entrepreneurship and Sustainability Issues*, 6/3 (2019), 1113–1126, http://dx.doi.org/10.9770/jesi.2019.6.3(4)

133   Beyond Meat, www.beyondmeat.com, accessed 9 October 2023

134   Tesla Solar Panels, www.tesla.com/solarpanels, accessed 9 October 2023

135   Ecovative, www.ecovative.com, accessed 9 October 2023

136   Onen, M, et al., "Nanosecond protonic programmable resistors for analog deep learning", *Science* 377 (29 July 2022), 539–543, https://mitibmwatsonailab.mit.edu/wp-content/uploads/2023/06/science.abp8064.pdf

137   Sangwan, VK and Hersam, MC, "Neuromorphic nanoelectronic materials", *Nature Nanotechnology*, 15/7 (2020), 517–528, https://doi.org/10.1038/s41565-020-0647-z

138   Ahmad, S and Scheinkman, L, "How can we be so dense? The benefits of using highly sparse representations", *arXiv* (2019), https://doi.org/10.48550/arXiv.1903.11257

139   BabyLM challenge, https://babylm.github.io, accessed 17 November 2023

140   Ye, X, Zhang, Z and Qiu, YL, "Review of application of high frequency smart meter data in energy economics and policy research", *Frontiers in Sustainable Energy Policy*, 2 (24 May 2023), https://doi.org/10.3389/fsuep.2023.1171093

141   Knayer, T and Kryvinska, N., "An analysis of smart meter technologies for efficient energy management in households and organizations", *Energy Reports*, 8 (November 2022), 4022–4040, https://doi.org/10.1016/j.egyr.2022.03.041

142   Budennyy, SA, et al., "Eco2AI: Carbon emissions tracking of machine learning models as the first step towards sustainable AI", *Doklady Mathematics*, 106/1 (December 2022), S118–S128, https://doi.org/10.1134/S1064562422060230

143   Roach, J, "Microsoft finds underwater datacenters are
       reliable, practical and use energy sustainably", *Microsoft*
       (14 September 2020), https://news.microsoft.com/source/
       features/sustainability/project-natick-underwater-
       datacenter, accessed 9 October 2023

144   de Jesus, C, "'Cryptomatoes' wants to recycle crypto
       mining heat to grow crops", *Coingeek* (13 March 2018),
       https://coingeek.com/cryptomatoes-wants-recycle-crypto-
       mining-heat-grow-crops, accessed 9 October 2023

145   Badea, L and Mungiu-Pupăzan, MC, "The economic
       and environmental impact of bitcoin", *IEEE Access*, 9
       (24 March 2021), 48091–48104, https://doi.org/10.1109/
       ACCESS.2021.3068636

146   Asgari, M, McDonald, MT and Pearce, JM, "Energy
       modeling and techno-economic feasibility analysis of
       greenhouses for tomato cultivation utilizing the waste
       heat of cryptocurrency miners", *Energies* 16/3 (2023), 1331,
       https://doi.org/10.3390/en16031331

147   MintGreen, https://mintgreen.co, accessed 9 October 2023

148   Heatmine, www.crunchbase.com/organization/heatmine,
       accessed 9 October 2023

Further Reading

Chapter 1

GapMinder, www.gapminder.org

Kende-Robb, CM, *Can the Poor Influence Policy? Participatory poverty assessments in the developing world* (The World Bank, 2002)

Chapter 2

Catapult Design, https://catapultdesign.org

Greenhouse Capital, https://greenhouse.capital

Target Global, https://targetglobal.vc

Chapter 3

Deep Learning Indaba, https://deeplearningindaba. com

European Patent Office, https://epo.org

Iceaddis, https://iceaddis.com

iHub Kenya, https://ihub.co.ke

Impact Hub Accra, https://accra.impacthub.net

MIT D-Lab, https://d-lab.mit.edu

Silicon Cape Initiative, https://siliconcape.com

Stanford Byers Center for Biodesign, https://biodesign.stanford.edu

Twende: Accelerating Social Innovation, https://twende.or.tz

United States Patent and Trademark Office, https://uspto.gov

Wennovation Hub, https://wennovationhub.org

Chapter 4

Frank's Hospital Workshop, www.frankshospitalworkshop.com

Global Disability Innovation Hub, https://disabilityinnovation.com

Hackteria, https://hackteria.org

Richards-Kortum, R, *Biomedical Engineering for Global Health* (Cambridge University Press, 2009)

Werner, D, Thuman, C and Maxwell, J, *Where There Is No Doctor: A village health care handbook* (Hesperian Foundation, 1977)

Chapter 6

Development & Approval Process, US Food & Drug Administration, https://fda.gov/drugs/development-approval-process-drugs

EUR-Lex CE medical device certification laws, https://eur-lex.europa.eu/eli/reg/2017/746/oj

European Medicines Agency, https://ema.europa.eu/en/human-regulatory/overview/medical-devices

Chapter 7

Alzheimer's Disease Neuroimaging Initiative (ADNI), https://adni.loni.usc.edu

Amazon Web Services, https://aws.amazon.com

California Consumer Privacy Act, https://oag.ca.gov/privacy/ccpa

Center for Biomedical Research Excellence (COBRE) initiative for schizophrenia, https://fcon_1000.projects.nitrc.org/indi/retro/cobre.html

D-Wave quantum cloud, https://dwavesys.com

Ensembl, https://ensembl.org

European Molecular Biology Laboratory's European Bioinformatics Institute (EMBL-EBI), https://ebi.ac.uk

GenBank Overview, National Library of Medicine, https://ncbi.nlm.nih.gov/genbank

General Data Protection Regulation, https://gdpr-info.eu

Health Insurance Portability and Accountability Act of 1996, https://cdc.gov/phlp/publications/topic/hipaa.html

National Center for Biotechnology Information (NCBI), https://ncbi.nlm.nih.gov

Parkinson's Progression Markers Initiative (PPMI), https://ppmi-info.org

Qiskit, https://qiskit.org/ (lessons and tutorial: https://youtube.com/@qiskit)

UCSC Genome Browser, https://genome.ucsc.edu

Chapter 8

Eco2AI, https://github.com/sb-ai-lab/Eco2AI

Kohler, C, "Ways To Repurpose Bitcoin Miner Heat" The Bitcoin Manual, https://thebitcoinmanual.com/articles/repurpose-bitcoin-miner-heat

Acknowledgments

I would like to extend my deepest gratitude to the many people who made this book possible.

First and foremost, I would like to thank my father, who after retirement slowly moved from teaching philosophy to not being interested at all in education. He made an exception by reading and commenting on this text.

I would like to thank the other people who gave me feedback during the writing: Peter and Victoria Gonchar for their in-depth comments and recommendations and Mirka Isomäki for the positive feedback and corrections.

Thanks to Harry Akligoh and Thomas Mboa Nkoudou for their kind words and comments.

I would like to mention also Joe Laredo for helping to shape the book's structure and introduction.

This text is full of many things, thoughts, and ideas coming from other books or other people I met along the way in my many years of work between Europe and Africa. It would be impossible to mention you all. For sure, the most enriching and enjoyable experience for me was the DocmeUp project and teaching at the African Institute for Mathematical Sciences. I had a lot of fun there. Travel and see.

The Author

 Dr Alessandro Crimi is a bio-medical engineer and health economist who alternated his career between neuroimaging and healthcare management in low-income countries.

He was born in Palermo, Italy. After completing his studies in engineering at the University of Palermo, he obtained a PhD in machine learning applied for medical imaging from the University of Copenhagen, and an MBA in healthcare management by the University of Basel.

Alessandro worked as post-doctoral researcher at the French Institute for Research in Computer Science (INRIA), Technical School of Switzerland (ETH Zurich), Italian Institute for Technology (IIT), and University Hospital of Zurich. In those institutes he made significant contributions to the field of computational neuroscience.

The post-doctoral years at European institutes were alternated by periods living in Ghana and other sub-Saharan countries, where Dr Crimi taught and carried out in-field projects about healthcare management. He taught for eight years at the African Institute for Mathematical Sciences (AIMS) in Ghana and South Africa on the machine learning in medicine course, where he also supervised numerous MSc theses. He has been the cofounder of a biotech startup operating between Ghana and Switzerland.

Dr Crimi since moved to Sano, the center for computational medicine in Poland, where as a research group leader, had to limit his engagements with AIMS to MSc thesis supervision. His teaching duties are mostly now related to AGH UST (University of Science and Technology in Krakow), where he is currently a professor. The projects he conducted in sub-Saharan Africa were related to prenatal care, diabetes, malaria, and HIV management, using novel technologies such as machine learning, image processing, and social engineering.

Dr Crimi is currently involved in initiatives to promote entrepreneurship among women and individuals with immigrant backgrounds, as well as technology transfer projects for young scientists.

⊕ www.alessandrocrimi.com

▦ www.linkedin.com/in/alecrimi

▣ https://twitter.com/Dr_Alex_Crimi